MERGERS

WITH THE BENEFIT OF

HINDSIGHT

ANNE HARNETTY

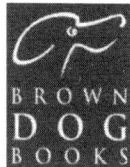

BROWN
DOG
BOOKS

Published under licence by Brown Dog Books and The Self-Publishing Partnership Ltd, 10b Greenway Farm, Bath Rd, Wick, nr. Bath BS30 5RL

www.selfpublishingpartnership.co.uk

ISBN printed book: 978-1-83952-442-4
ISBN e-book: 978-1-83952-443-1

Cover design by Kevin Rylands
Internal design by Tim Jollands

Printed and bound in the UK

This book is printed on FSC® certified paper

MIX
Paper | Supporting
responsible forestry
FSC
www.fsc.org   FSC® C013604

MERGERS

WITH THE BENEFIT OF

HINDSIGHT

Contents

Introduction

Following hours of research, speaking to Managing Partners, CEOs, Senior Partners and COOs of over twenty professional service firms ranging in turnover from £10 million to £800 million in the top legal 200 London and regionally that had completed some fifty mergers between them, I was encouraged by many to write a book that incorporated the findings. All had been involved in either mergers or acquisitions dating from 2012 to 2020. Full-service law firms and those with niche specialisations. We have followed the consistent themes that emerged from our research. We wanted to give an insight into what happens once a merger or acquisition is signed, and we wanted it to be a guide that would be read because it is based on the personal experiences of others who have been generous with their time and brutally frank. At the start of the research, we wondered what would be raised, had the issues we read about evolved or remained the same, because so many firms have gone through the merger and acquisition process and yet so many are deemed to be unsuccessful, with the same recurring issues, the same issues that appear in every article written about the process: was there a way we could help change that?

With the gift of hindsight, what had been learned and what practical advice could those that have been through it offer? Throughout this book priority is given to their thoughts and experiences: if we agree with them or not, they have lived them. I hope that the benefit of hindsight is exactly that for all those who are considering going through this undertaking. If it does, those that have given their time can certainly save you hours of problems that they have faced and learned from. Every quote made is from a Managing Partner, Senior Partner, CEO or COO who has really been fully involved with the M&A proposition. Some were happy to be quoted, others preferred to remain anonymous but everything they shared has equal value.

All the firms we spoke to were happy to share the good, the bad, the shockingly unexpected and the myths that perpetuate, and the exhaustion that comes with the merger process. A Managing Partner told us very clearly that ego got in the way of what was needed, and perhaps we all have that voice in our head that says we can do it better, but do we?

Robin Sharma the Canadian writer stated, 'The real trick in life is to turn hindsight into foresight that reveals insight.'

We hope this research helps you do just that because in each of the chapters we outline an issue and then follow this with anecdotal evidence from firms that have experienced such issues. Quotations are given to support this evidence, looking at assumptions that were made and leading to what was learned in hindsight and a case study.

We have listened to the experience of other experts in their field and asked them to contribute.

Peter Noyce, Head of Legal Sector at Menzies LLP and author of Brighter Thinking For Law Firms.

David Sparkes, founder and CEO Millbourn Ross.

Paul McCluskey, Managing Director of Gemstone Legal who helps law firms to improve their approach to banking, finance and risk management.

Clive Knott, IT Consultant.

Doug McPherson, owner of 10½ Boots.

Martin Soulsby, Director Jonson Beaumont.

They all offer practical advice relevant to the merger and acquisition process, and I would like to thank them all for their contribution to this guide. I would also like to dedicate this work to Ian Harvey, who sadly died in April 2021, having encouraged me to start Jonson Beaumont Core and who was integral to the business.

CHAPTER I

The M&A market

M&A activity has been making the headlines weekly in the legal press in 2021 with some thirteen mergers already in the first half of the year. The Law Gazette stated that this is expected to remain high for the next three years. This follows on from strong activity in 2020, but what is driving that activity? The Covid pandemic focussed minds and has forced firms to cut costs in property, support staff and non-efficient fee earners, making them hungry for business growth, developing specialist areas, the opportunity to cross-sell, to expand geographically and to diversify as 89 percent of law firms reported notable increases in income. Large law firms are the least active in the M&A market because they have reached the scale they need to service their UK clients and would only be looking for global opportunities. For the mid-tier it is a very different story. They are squeezed from top firms who will look to gain their more profitable clients and from smaller firms who are looking to grow their own market share by gaining geographic reach and competing heavily on price and specialisation that offers a more personal service. The mid-tier and smaller firms also face an ageing population. In 2017 The Solicitors Regulatory Authority produced a survey of 180,000 solicitors of whom 21 per cent were aged between 55 and 64. There is a real issue in succession planning in the bottom half of the legal top 200 which drives partners to search for earn-out opportunities. Younger fee earners do not always aspire to be partners where they have to invest in equity; for them it is an old-fashioned concept, and new entrants to the legal market, often as limited companies, have shown that they can offer high-level salaries that are not dependant on the billable hour and allow quality of life and the ability to practice law in a way that younger fee earners find more accommodating to their lifestyle aspirations.

There is also the issue of professional indemnity insurance, with two-thirds of firms renewing on 1 Oct. The pressure this year is immense, with an increase in insurance cost up by 10–30 percent. In smaller firms with turnover up to

£10 million this cost often drives managing partners towards exiting by retiring, selling, or seeking an MBO. With so many firms seeking opportunities to merge or acquire it is no wonder that multiple conversations between firms take place whilst they seek the right match as they look for the same opportunities as their competitors. Andrew Roberts of Ampersand Legal comments: 'Fees for brokers, accountants and lawyers can appear to be a barrier to sale, but the costs of the alternative such as run-off, redundancies, and storage are often far higher. If the firm is a good business there will always be others happy to acquire it, it is only the dynamics of the deal you need to get right.'

Merge or acquire?

What are the clear differences between a merger and an acquisition? A merger occurs when two separate entities combine forces to create a new, joint organisation. Meanwhile, an acquisition refers to the takeover of one entity by another, which usually involves the acquired company operating under the parent company's name. The reality is that the lines blur between the two and very few mergers are equal, and one firm is very likely to be dominant, which needs to be accepted. However, for PR purposes it is politely disguised as a merger, so everyone feels better.

'We never say that we are acquiring a firm, we are humans not things to acquire.' PRAGNESH MODHWADIA, MANAGING PARTNER AXIOM DWFM

Our research suggested that even acquisitive firms who had gone through the M&A process several times did so with varying levels of success, as they tried to appease their merger partners or lost sight of an integration plan.

We recognise that knowledge and expertise are not the same thing. Most firms have gained knowledge about every step of the merger or acquisition process but as often as not, that knowledge is not applied. From the very beginning of the merger or acquisition journey you need a clear strategy because successful understanding of the purpose of the merger or acquisition is key. Too often in our research it was surprising that several mergers and acquisitions had no robust planning at all, there was no analysis as to what advantage a merger or acquisition would bring and if the other party were looking for similar gains. In fact, there was no analysis, but there was often a reliance on talking to firms and people that were known to partners, often in a similar location, who have a lightbulb moment that they should merge because they know one another. The start of the merger process is pushed forward on 'gut instinct' by managing partners who are well acquainted, and there is an assumption that a merger or acquisition will work, and it might, as long as the strategy does not just become a desire to merge or acquire rather than a thorough, analysed plan with a desired outcome that has tangible benefits to both firms. Remember to continually assess where the value creation is in any M&A deal. Mergers and acquisitions are a serious undertaking, not a knee-jerk reaction. They take a long time to 'bed in', and with so much to consider it is not surprising that firms often struggle to make a success of a merger or acquisition, however compelling their original strategy assessment was. It is a delicate balance to get merger or acquisition and subsequent integration right and you should remain true to your criteria for the merger and constantly return to those criteria.

A successful merger or acquisition should begin with a clear expression of the reasons for doing it, or why would the firm undertake the cost and risk of merging or acquiring? What it is you are trying to achieve? What will success look like? What are your objectives, and will they be met if you merge? You need a purpose and vision to aid success. The vision needs to be better than both legacy firms, with new values and goals for the newly merged business. Merger is not a strategy: it is a tactic which supports your strategy and that needs a realistic plan. Firms who had been aggressive in their acquisition strategy still had failures and found integration was not always easy. The benefits of a merger or acquisition need to be expressed clearly and link to the overall strategy to ensure partners understand why they should support their managing partners' vision and ideas, because when mergers or acquisitions work the benefits are profound. With a merger or acquisition plan outlined, this document can form the basis of a blueprint that builds as all aspects of the M&A deal are considered and analysed.

The firms we spoke to in our research had been looking for a merger or acquisition partner for several years and most firms had entered several discussions before finding the right synergy with their eventual M&A partners. Their considerations included cultural fit, financial fit, operational fit and strategic fit. With any merger or acquisition change will happen, and because there is an expectation that things are bound to be different, change becomes more acceptable as people are ready to embrace new things, and firms must plan to ensure that those changes go through. This could be the catalyst for positive transformation that may have been wanted for some time.

Common reasons to merge or acquire

We heard numerous reasons to merge or acquire, but what were the broader business goals? Firms wanted to take on more complex work with their existing clients or wanted to be able to pitch and win work they would not have been considered for pre-merger or acquisition. They wanted to be able to have a full service offering because their clients wanted greater strength and depth and fear of losing clients drove M&A.

Geographical alignment featured strongly, extending territories in complementary areas with complementary services. Some firms stated that it was hard to grow in a particular location by trying to take on lateral hires, and by extending geographically they had a different offering for clients. Firms wanted to strengthen areas of the business, gaining deeper expertise in weaker areas and to further strengthen areas that were doing well. Certainly, to develop capability in given areas. Several regional firms wanted to increase their profile by having a foothold in London, sometimes as a gateway to international work, or to offer clients a London service with regional cost benefits.

Attracting and retaining staff because the joint entity was now of a size that offered a clear career path, better clients, and more complex work was considered a major benefit of M&A. This applied to both fee-earning and support staff.

Several firms wanted to enhance, re-enforce, and cement their ranking in the top 100 UK law firms.

Accelerated growth was another benefit rather than trying to grow organically or after several bolt-ons. An ageing partner population saw M&A as providing an exit plan for partners who wanted to retire, who had not considered or who had failed at succession planning and would have the considerable cost of run-off if they wound up the firm.

Sadly, there are firms that are acquired from the administrators and sole practitioners who have died and their practice is taken over.

We also heard of peripheral reasons for merging; just because you have capacity in your building and the merger partner is coming to the end of their lease you can reduce your combined property cost base. However, are you on the same page with other key criteria that will benefit your plan for merging, because otherwise what you have is a convenience of property rather than a vision that your partners will embrace. Your statement of objectives and understanding the purpose to merge or acquire is key to success so that partners will identify with those needs.

How else will you ensure success?

Acquiring firms were also on a learning curve. However, once they had gone through several acquisitions they stated that key to their success was centred around getting to know new colleagues and ensuring staff at all levels were integrated by combining teams. It must be remembered that new teams have quite possibly not met and do not know the style of work that their new colleagues have, and that has to be facilitated.

One managing partner in the south-east said that to ensure people feel part of a new entity he got them out of their old building quickly because when they move office they feel and act as part of something new that they are proud of. For some firms that is not possible because of costs, but you must mix teams to ensure they come together; do not leave people sitting in the same place with the same people because that is still two separate entities and does not encourage cohesion.

Acquisitive firms also ensured that they moved immediately to a combined IT system, believing it did not work as well if on day one there are several systems in play.

'We insist the firm we are acquiring move to our IT systems, we put in IT trainers from day one to deal with any potential issues. The changes are just a consequence of acquisition, but you can re-train for something different.' MANAGING PARTNER REGIONAL LAW FIRM

Regardless of a merger or acquisition there was agreement amongst the firms we spoke to that you must act quickly on difficult decisions and be honest, then you will win hearts and minds. People will lose their roles but be supportive. Roles may well change and reporting lines to new heads of department will happen, but ensure that you have open communication. Do not allow salaries to become an area of contention – agree them beforehand so there is no argument and ensure that there is a salary discussion for all roles. Not everyone will be happy but remove dissenters quickly: the firm you merge or acquire with usually have a list of people they believe will be an issue. Do not fudge it, move forward and use key people to champion the new entity.

Let clients know what is happening by communicating and sending consistent messages to them. Reassure them that your letterhead will change and yes, you will have a different email address, but more importantly your service levels will be refined and sharpened and that you are there to support them. It is important they know that you are now offering a broader and deeper resource but that their relationship is unchanged. Ask them for measured feedback post-M&A. You are a relationship business and clients need to know that their views matter to you.

What assumptions were made and with hindsight what was learned?

'Plan, plan and plan again and when you think you have done enough planning, plan again on every single thing.' CEO TOP 50 LAW FIRM

Do not assume that the changes that come with any M&A are effortless or that they are easily sustainable. Just because you appear to be of like minds it does not follow that everything will come together easily. With a merger or acquisition everything changes both operationally and culturally and as a result, mergers and acquisitions challenge everything from day-to-day work, the purpose, leadership and even the firm's identity.

'Merger is a step forward, but not the magic wand that will solve everything.' MANAGING PARTNER REGIONAL LAW FIRM

Do not have a concept, have a project plan. Remember the purpose for merging or acquiring and do not merge just because you know another firm and like them. Really get to the bottom of what the benefit is to merge or acquire, and remember it takes months of discussions. Even when those red flags were raised many just felt unable to walk away, especially after the time they had invested and the fatigue they were feeling.

'We thought we could make it work; we had a sense that it didn't smell right but had taken so long we were exhausted.'
MANAGING PARTNER REGIONAL LAW FIRM

Ego can get in the way for several reasons, but it can and does occlude common sense. It might feel like failure to walk away and once it hits the legal press, which it inevitably does, it might be slightly embarrassing, but if your due diligence and other investigations reveal that you are not a good match then you can have an amicable split. In reality many merger talks break down. It will save you time, effort and money if you walk away. Instead, we listen to that voice in our head that says we can do it. There is a common assumption that with M&A comes profit, and it will come if you have followed every aspect of due diligence and there are no hidden issues that impact profitability.

Recognise what as a firm you have to offer before you consider M&A, because the issues you face will not be solved by a merger or acquisition unless you get your house in order first before going to market. Does the firm you are targeting fit you strategically, culturally, financially and operationally?

'We had to take a major look at ourselves from top to bottom, literally everything we did and how we did it. We brought in a consultancy to help us. It brought rewards because instead of looking at smaller firms to acquire, we really did know ourselves and could look for more substantial partners.' MANAGING PARTNER TOP 200 LAW FIRM

Once you have got yourself in the best possible shape it is not the best hypothesis that you can do everything yourself, in a given timescale whilst carrying on business as usual. A merger broker can be hugely helpful in the introduction of firms you may not have considered. They will look at your aims and match firms to you without being assumptive. The most quoted reason for using a broker was because the firm remained anonymous through initial forays on match. Best use of time was also high on the list because, whilst partners can conduct research or already know firms that they want to approach, it saves valuable management time in both the research and approach phases. Whilst larger firms have the resource to access public data on firms with turnover in excess of £14m there is very little publicly available data with firms with revenue up to £14m. Using a broker with a deep dataset is advantageous and provides a quicker route to conversations. A broker does have applied knowledge and critical thinking about why a merger will benefit both parties with a focussed target list. They can also help give an exciting vision of the benefits of merging with a larger firm, rather than the 'you know you want to join us' approach, which only reflects the benefits to the acquirer. There is a strange misconception that regional firms, compared to their London counterparts, are somehow not as good, are poorly run and must be excited by merging with a London firm. The reality is often very different; regional firms have often invested in and become early adaptors of new technology and in their growth trajectory have invested in high quality operational heads. They have lost arcane practices, the need to store miles of paperwork that is never looked at but has huge cost, the servers still on site instead of in the cloud. Above all they are more often than not more profitable than those they are looking to merge with. It is not reality that all London firms are all modern architecture, technically leading lights and highly profitable.

'In my naivety I thought every London firm was like Suits on TV, glass, chrome and totally efficient, and I was amazed by the lack of investment we encountered when looking for an acquisition partner.'
MANAGING PARTNER SE LAW FIRM

'Have a strategy not an opportunistic approach. Using a broker makes it more strategic and organised.' MANAGING PARTNER SE REGIONAL LAW FIRM

'We should have had more clarity on the future direction of the firm after we merged. The strategy was to merge but there was nothing beyond that and we didn't think enough about what the future might look like.'
CEO LONDON LAW FIRM

So many firms in our research thought they could do it as well and without the cost of a project director and project team. Why on earth would they need an outside team and the inherent cost? Larger firms can put together a dedicated project team, but smaller firms find that hard to do. Is it fair that your Managing Partner, who may never have been involved in a merger or acquisition before, must manage business as usual, bill, deal with every other issue within the firm and run the complexity of a merger, with its myriad issues? If too many partners are involved and consensus of opinion is being sought, lethargy insidiously creeps in either from fear, lack of understanding or information and stalls out decision making. Lawyers love advising others, but they prevaricate when they must make decisions about their own firm.

'The trouble with lawyers is that they often have a conversation in their own head that isn't reality.' MANAGING PARTNER LONDON LAW FIRM

A project director, with the authority to act, can help set the agenda for integration because they are experienced in assimilating every area of the business, they have seen the pitfalls before and so can guide you out of them. They are there to help break deadlocks that will inevitably occur when firms merge. Deadlocks slow momentum and often hamper mergers. A project director will anticipate problems, solve them and move forward.

'I wish I'd known that people like you existed so we had a project director when we started this process.' MANAGING PARTNER SE FIRM

Engage a project team so you can release your partners to get on with what they do best and do not let them get into the minutiae of the deal process. Once the deal is done, mergers fail so often because partners running it cannot face the barrage of decisions that have to be made and the constant need to keep everyone on side. Remember, merger fatigue is real not an imagined concept.

'It was more successful than I dared to dream of and so much harder than I ever thought. I did not realise the total exhaustion.'
MANAGING PARTNER REGIONAL LAW FIRM

Even with the best project team in place do not believe that the M&A journey will be a quick one once Heads of Terms have been signed. Integration is where some of the hardest issues arise. Not everyone will recognise that there is always a dominant party in M&A, and because you are close in culture does not mean that everyone will be in agreement on all the issues you will have to focus on.

Another myth is that staff at all levels will be overjoyed by the prospect of M&A because they will understand that it brings new opportunities for them as individuals and the firms as a whole. If you have not sold the concept to staff and do not continue to give them positive messages to keep them on side, top talent will look for external opportunities. Your staff will see changes, from where they sit and with whom, to who they report to, even down to where they eat their lunch. New processes, however small, are a challenge and can cause real anxiety with staff. Remember the impact on people at all levels, they might be elated, excited or scared. It is a journey that people need to understand so they are comfortable with it, and they can then embrace it.

Communication is key, so the messages that support the purpose for the merger or acquisition need to be regular and they need to excite everyone as to why it will be a better firm at the end of it.

'The key reason strategic initiatives fail is because they are not sufficiently exciting to generate the energy and commitment needed to overcome the problems that will arise on the journey.' CEO TOP 100 LAW FIRM

Partners and staff need to be kept informed and on side. Find the key reasons to merge and explain that vision to your partners and keep referring to it so you continually engage them with the vision you started with. The research highlighted that if there were fractures in the partner group they did not become apparent until after the deal had been completed. This is often because of cultural differences in communication and management style; some firms are very open in their communication style; others are closed and secretive.

'It is the hardest thing you will ever do in your life: to say it was hard would be an understatement.' MANAGING PARTNER LONDON LAW FIRM

Case study
An acquisitive firm now command how and when the firm they are acquiring is informed because in their first acquisition their cultural style was to keep their staff fully informed at each stage as to what was happening and when. The firm that they were acquiring did not inform their staff of anything and the first the

staff knew of the acquisition was when they heard it announced on local radio on the day of the merger.

In our research we heard of attitude issues in both fee earners and partners and conversely, we heard that a firm quickly got rid of dissenters because they affected so much of what was good.

'You need to immerse yourself in the firm so that they know you. We are a hearts and minds business, and you have no chance if you don't understand that.' MANAGING PARTNER LEADING REGIONAL LAW FIRM

Case study

Costs had not been anticipated by one acquiring firm where efficiencies were very different. Photocopier contracts tied into individual photocopiers, contracts which were never assessed and always renewed but which were totally inefficient and hugely expensive. Excessive storage costs, where their office was paperless and the acquired firm were not, in a storage space that had not been reviewed for years. Not only did they inherit the cost of storage, they had to invest hundreds of man hours opening everything in storage, trying to trace owners or their descendants, and decide what to do with the contents which were not always straightforward paperwork and included clothing and ceremonial robes and original manuscripts for plays.
MANAGING PARTNER LONDON LAW FIRM

Case study

It is sometimes inevitable that staff that you would have preferred to stay move on. However, it can sometimes be addressed. A partner left shortly after one acquisition because he did not agree with what he assumed was happening with the firm he had spent many years and had invested so much time in. He quickly asked to return because he was not enjoying the firm he joined and did not feel he was fitting in with their culture, and having heard from his old peers that actually, the merged firm was meeting their expectations. He now promotes the realities of working in an acquired firm with partners of firms that are being acquired to help them settle into the new environment. He is happy to explain that if people allow things to settle down, they will see that the changes are for the better.
MANAGING PARTNER FULL-SERVICE REGIONAL LAW FIRM

CHAPTER 2

The benefits of a merger broker

During this chapter we will explore the advantages to be gained by organisations using a sector specialist M&A broker.

Once a leadership team or organisation has agreed a strategy, the next phase of the process will need careful consideration about delivering the strategy and ultimately what resources will be required to ensure success. Whether the organisation is looking to scale through acquisition or mergers, or looking to identify the options for a successful exit, using a sector specialist M&A broker should be on your list of considerations.

Time and expertise are the obvious benefits to be gained from instructing a sector specialist M&A broker. As we discuss the options available and highlight the benefits to using a merger broker, we will also explore best practice when engaging with your merger broker and aim to provide a foundation for ensuring a successful partnership.

What are my options?

Professional services firms have long been committed to a strategy of organic growth. In a mature market the war for talent, desire for new clients and the battle for market share all present significant challenges to an organic growth strategy.

M&A is not a strategy in itself, but a mechanism for achieving a strategic goal. For those firms whose strategy requires scaling through M&A it is important not to underestimate the significant time and financial investment required. Preparation is singularly the most important thing that defines the success of a transaction.

When it comes to M&A strategy, professional services firms display a broad spectrum of behaviours. The range includes firms who are committed to an organic growth strategy, and as a by-product have a preference for being reactive or more opportunistic to conversations that come their way through to very proactive firms who have a defined methodology for creating targeted conversations, and thus generating an active pipeline of conversations on an ongoing basis. In the middle of this range are those firms who are proactively committed to an M&A strategy, often utilising the services of sector specialist M&A brokers.

It is essential that you are clear about the approach that suits your firm. This is not to say that the approach cannot be taken up or down a gear depending on priorities or needs. Only a small proportion of firms are consistently building their M&A pipeline in order to complete regular transactions during the year. More commonly firms that complete larger transactions will not repeat the process quickly as the focus moves to integration.

Before you begin the process to sell/exit, merge or acquire, you will want to take a view on how you approach it. At one end of the spectrum that can mean DIY and at the other outsourcing the mandate to a consultant/advisor or specialist M&A broker.

Your M&A approach

There are a number of ways in which you can approach the search or origination process for finding a suitable acquisition, merger partner or acquirer.

The three things that will determine your M&A approach will be;

- Investment
- Speed
- Capacity

Financial investment

What's your appetite to invest financially in the search process?

- Firms at the opportunistic end of the spectrum are far less likely to invest. This clearly has its advantages in terms of cost and upfront outlay, but equally may have some disadvantages in terms of speed and capacity.

- Those firms that chose to invest in a sector specialist M&A broker or another consultant/advisor to proactively conduct a search project may benefit from the level of conversations they can be exposed to, as well as accelerating to a desired outcome.

- Like any investment, it's important to consider the potential for return on that investment. Does abstaining from investing in a third party prohibit the opportunity for growth? Every strategy ultimately requires investment, so you should be considering what you are prepared to invest in order to deliver on your strategy, and what the success of that strategy looks like for the business and its owners.

Speed

How fast do you want/need a transaction to happen?

- Clearly at the pre-pack end of the market, speed is everything – as the firm in question will likely have a finite period of existence. However, speed is not always a good thing if you 'have' to do a transaction. More often than not, you will want to take the right time to find the right partner and you should be cognisant that judgement can be impaired by the need for speed.

- Ultimately the speed of a transaction will likely depend on how quickly and regularly you want conversations to take place, and this will probably be determined by the scale of your ambition.

- One thing to consider is the time it takes to complete an M&A transaction. This is dependent on a number of factors including the regularity of communications between parties, speed at which information is shared and the focus and desire to complete the transaction in a timely manner. Depending on the size and complexity of the transaction, you should be expecting a minimum of six months and anything up to two years for a completion. With this in mind, the prospect of accelerating introductions and the process through a sector specialist M&A broker becomes a serious consideration.

Capacity

How much time can you and the equity/leadership team dedicate to the process?

- It is well documented that managing partners/CEOs and leadership teams can struggle to maintain a cadence of activity against a growth strategy that includes any aspect of M&A, as they are often, quite rightly, prioritising the day-to-day running of the business.

- If you choose to be very proactive about your M&A strategy, it's important not to underestimate the impact that may have on your time and that of your colleagues. Having a sector specialist M&A broker can be very helpful in filtering the communications and insulating you from some of the administrative side of the transaction and keeping you focussed on the important areas.

- This inevitably always plays out better for senior/managing partners that do not have fee-earning responsibilities or those firms that can allocate dedicated resources to delivering the M&A strategy.

Once you have drawn some conclusions on your appetite for investment, need for speed and capacity to participate in an M&A project, then you can consider the options available to you for delivering on your strategy.

Do it yourself

The obvious benefit of a DIY approach is that it limits your financial exposure to consulting or success fees, or both. Your existing professional advisors such as accountant, bank or insurer, may be in a position to recommend to you some firms from within their network for consideration, and using internal resources you may be able to build up a clear picture of target firms with whom you may want to engage in conversation.

A DIY approach is often easier when you have some internal resource that can be applied to an M&A project. Herein lies the dilemma, because smaller firms often don't have the additional internal resource available to utilise on a discreet project or have the appetite for financial investment in a third party. An increasing number of firms who are very proactive in M&A have introduced an M&A manager /director to the business to support this aspect of their growth.

If you do choose the DIY approach, there are a number of key considerations and resources that you should be exploring, including:

- What sources are available for referral or introduction to potential target firms? i.e. partners/lawyers within the firm or other professional advisors connected to the firm.

- What resources does the business have available to support and manage the project?

- What public domain data sources are available to create a target list? i.e. Companies House, Legal 500, The Law Society 'Find a Solicitor', SRA database, legal-target.com, etc?

- What methodology are you going to apply to research, identification, targeting, approach and engagement?

- Who is going to support and guide your due diligence process?

- What professional advisors are you going to use?

One potential downside of a DIY approach is that your options may be restricted by the depth and breadth of the research you are able to conduct, or indeed by the polarised view of the referral or introductory sources you use. It is not uncommon to hear of M&A targets being discounted because one lawyer has an opinion on another lawyer from said firm. Obtaining a broad and in-depth view of the market can increase your exposure to relevant conversations.

Benefits of using a sector specialist M&A broker

If you have come to the conclusion that delivering against your firm's strategy requires a proactive approach to M&A, there are a number of benefits to using a sector specialist M&A expert.

- **Time** Instructing an experienced M&A broker has multiple benefits when it comes to time.
  - o It allows a Managing Partner and other senior leadership the freedom to prioritise the day-to-day running of the business,

without compromising the speed at which they can deliver against the firm's strategy.

o   Once an experienced M&A broker understands the mandate and has clarity on your search criteria, they will be in a position to accelerate the connections to decision makers within firms and ultimately the outcome you require.

- **Momentum** Without doubt one of the key benefits to working with a skilled M&A broker is their ability to maintain momentum in conversations. Without focus and regular attention, conversations can drift or even break down, which is unhelpful to all parties concerned. Having an advisor to maintain the momentum benefits all parties. Some 'fast fail' logic can be applied to M&A conversations. That is not to suggest you set out looking for them to fail, but move quickly and be decisive, and the quicker you find a fail point, the quicker you can move onto more beneficial conversations. Spending 3-9 months in conversations that fail is wasting valuable time.

- **Market data** An M&A broker will likely have a deep and comprehensive dataset, over and above anything that might be available in the public domain, that provides the foundation for accelerated research, analysis, identification and outreach.

- **Market insight** A sector specialist M&A broker spends most of their time speaking to firms in the market place, which provides them with unparalleled market insight and understanding. As a result, they are in a position to provide a holistic view of the wider market conditions in addition to a potentially more rounded and impartial perspective on target firms. This can be helpful when communicating internally with stakeholders who hold a particular view on a target firm/s.

- **Anonymity** A market outreach campaign via an M&A broker provides early-stage anonymity, which is often highly valued in professional services firms. Firms who are looking to sell/exit naturally want to be very discreet and discerning as to whom they engage with in order to protect their identity and ultimately their business. Whilst some acquisitive firms are very open about their consolidation aspirations, others prefer to be more discreet about their strategic growth.

- **Preparation and outreach** If it's the first time you're selling a law firm and not sure where to look for buyers, then a sector specialist M&A broker is well placed to give you advice on preparing your firm to sell and also access to a broad range of acquisitive firms and organisations. This same logic applies for firms looking to acquire/ merge.

- **Negotiating** A sector specialist M&A broker will be an experienced negotiator and plays a valuable role in the negotiation process, as well as protecting both parties from difficult conversations.

- **Creating the value proposition** An M&A broker will be able to support you in creating a compelling narrative around the benefits of merger/acquisition or disposal. The value of this story-telling piece cannot be underestimated in early-stage conversations and is often the foundation on which conversations are built.

Best practice for engaging with a specialist M&A broker

Once you have decided to engage a specialist M&A broker, you should be thinking about preparing yourself for the process. The M&A broker will be able to provide some advice and guidance on preparing the firm for conversations. This applies if you are looking for sale/exit or acquisition/ merger conversations.

As we said at the start of this chapter, preparation is singularly the most important thing that defines the success of a transaction. In this sense, preparation is primarily about preparing the business for M&A. Planning ahead for due diligence on your firm is vitally important and will help you to discover and resolve any potential pain points that may surface during a due diligence process.

At its highest level, preparation will include a review and understanding of the following areas of the business:

- Financial
- Insurance
- Property
- Workforce
- Corporate governance
- Online
- Technology
- Suppliers
- Clients
- Miscellaneous

In addition to the preparation piece, there are a number of behaviours and approaches that will enhance your experience working with a broker, including:

- **Transparency** Being clear and transparent with your broker about your strategy and motivations for M&A is fundamentally important to the process. Strategic drivers for an M&A transaction can be varied and not always about purely growth. For some firms it may be a defensive move to sustain or protect a particular area of work or specialist skills, and for another it may be a move to mitigate any vulnerability to panel reviews. Whatever the drivers, it's very important to articulate this to your broker, so they can secure conversations that meet your criteria for a successful outcome.

- **Communication** Ensuring you have regular planned reviews and that you are readily available for questions will help with the momentum of conversations. Timely responses to emails and communications sets a positive tone for the process between you and the M&A broker and also other third parties.

- **Deal with pain points** It's inevitable that you may have any host of pain points that will surface during conversations with third parties. These could be anything from a high performing partner whose views are not aligned with the strategy, or significant loans or debt the business has incurred. Raising these with your broker at the outset and agreeing on the best approach to resolving and communicating will be essential during the process.

Embracing all these points will ensure a successful partnership between you and your broker.

Selecting other professional advisors

Once you have defined your strategy and are confident that M&A will deliver the outcomes you are looking to achieve, you have chosen the approach and potentially selected a specialist M&A broker, you should be thinking about the other professional advisors you will need to facilitate the process.

It's common for firms to use their existing primary professional advisors i.e. accountant, bank, insurer, solicitor. However, it is worth considering the experience and knowledge of each advisor as it relates to the transaction. You may find another professional advisor has more relevant experience, which can be invaluable during a transaction.

This can be particularly true when it comes to valuations of professional services firms, negotiations on partnership deeds and advice around professional indemnity insurance and successor practice regulations.

Advisors to consider:

- Accountant
- Bank
- Solicitor
- Insurance

Not all your professional advisors will play a part from the outset of your transaction, but it's recommended to keep key advisors appraised of your plans at an early stage. The sooner your advisors are aware, the better prepared they can be to support you when required.

Some advisors may also be able to contribute to your M&A strategy and the search process

CHAPTER 3

Culture

'Cultural fit is important, but what predicts success most is the rate at which employees adapt as organisational culture changes over time. The best cultures encourage diversity to drive innovation but are anchored in shared core beliefs.' THE HARVARD BUSINESS REVIEW

How important is culture and is it a barrier to success? Certainly, our research showed that it is one of the biggest obstacles in merger integration because of the conflict a clash of culture raises. If you discover that your firm's values and cultural styles are incompatible, mergers often fail.

Culture is easy to sense and hard to measure, it is a soft concept and people do find it a challenge to recognise their own culture. Everything from the physical environment to how you use language can be telling in terms of cultural styles. Are your aesthetics modern and contemporary or more classic, are you paperless or not? Language is important in a business because it helps paint a picture of an organisation's culture. Do you only refer to lawyers and partners on your web site, or do you include your key business operational heads? Do you refer to non-lawyers as 'other staff', because a small change in words can have a big impact on how things are perceived.

Outsiders often have a better insight because cultural givens are not implicit to them, which is why a project director can be helpful. We often heard statements like this:

'Let's face it, we are all lawyers with similar interests so we knew we would get on, and of course knew that everything would be fine.'
CEO TOP 100 LONDON LAW FIRM

As the integration progressed, however, cultural differences really emerged and were hard to work through, so firms need to understand culture in a more nuanced way. One Managing Partner told us that they had merged with firms who have a totally different culture and age dynamic but their mindset and ambitions were aligned so that they could evolve a culture that works because they are all ambitious for the new firm. We also had a firm who looked at culture differently because they believed that partners of long standing of twenty-plus years get entrenched in the way that they practice law, and you cannot change that, but if you look at a bottom-up culture with younger fee earners that you bring in, especially new joiners, they can give them a vision of what it is they want to achieve and they have the aspiration to help them make that happen.

'When you first meet, people are charm itself. Then you merge and their true colours show. People who were acquired referred to us as 'that lot'.'
MANAGING PARTNER REGIONAL LAW FIRM

Cultural measures are often dependent on employee surveys and questionnaires, which are not always reliable. Culture is a combination of factors that create the work environment, but what does culture mean? Do you recognise your own firm's culture and what your firm stands for? Are you prepared to change what is fundamentally key to you to fit in with your merger partner's cultural style and attributes? How well-aligned are you in your cultural beliefs, and are both parties open to change?

How do you view strategy, innovation, collaboration, knowledge, marketing and pricing? How do you as a firm treat your staff and clients? Do you recognise your staff as your most important asset, or do you only recognise fee-earning staff? No merger is easy if you are opposed on cultural issues because cultural differences cause tensions in staff. Those tensions can lead to a drop in morale and loss of staff, who leave because they have not been shown a new cultural vision. You need to take the best cultural aspects from both firms and align them.

"You need a joint purpose and vision from day one on the table not a fixation on finance." MANAGING PARTNER REGIONAL LAW FIRM

Every firm inevitably told me that they have a collegiate culture, but whilst that is nice to say, it is not reality. I have encountered democracies, autocracies, hierarchies and meritocracies. Each has its place and needs to be recognised to get the best out of individuals. The certainty in a merger is the need to collaborate to ensure integration is effective, to form new teams, to cross-sell and ultimately to deliver the promised vision of the merged firm both internally and externally. To achieve this, management must articulate what the firm's culture is so they can define it to everyone, because it is something that everyone in the firm contributes to. Decide what values, beliefs and behaviours you want as part of your culture: it is unlikely that you will always agree on everything but agree on the basics and what is really important, including how you treat one another.

If you are unable to define it, how can your staff contribute to the behaviours that you want to see reflected in your culture? In a newly merged firm, you must decide what makes your culture distinctive. What is it that partners value in that culture, how do staff connect to it and how will it benefit clients?

It is likely that the new vision for the merged entity will find a change in culture, which people will embrace if it is a shared vision because it gives them a sense of identity. Culture can be used to obfuscate other issues and, when both parties walk away, they quote cultural differences, but there is no doubt that if you fail to recognise what it is you have, those differences can affect the process.

'Cultural fit was the number one priority. We went more by instinct and gut feel and the spirit in which discussions were conducted. It's hard to know what your culture is.' COO TOP 100 LAW FIRM

Does culture have to match? Most firms we interviewed had culture as their number one priority and the hardest to objectively assess. I have read numerous articles as to why there must be a cultural match, or the merger will fail. The reality is that there is no such thing as a perfect match but you can be as well-matched as you possibly can be. There is no doubt that you must be very aware of cultural differences and behavioural norms to overcome any challenges and ensure common goals are met.

Leaders on both sides often fail to recognise what they actually have in terms of culture, but they have a perception of what they have.

Firms were happy to say they had no cultural measures at all, that they had a superficial approach rather than a forensic test of any kind, they had dinners and spoke and found that they had a lot in common, was the general measure for culture.

Those firms we interviewed for the report believed that there must be an understanding of the cultural styles in play. This was highlighted in the ways decisions were made. What is your decision-making style? Is it consensus-driven or top-down? It is important to understand because integration needs quick decisions and decisive thoughts. Different styles lead to slow decision making or the failure to make or implement decisions, and difficulties will arise if you cannot implement new strategies. It is not the time to procrastinate when some staff will inevitably know that they will not be part of the merged firm moving forward.

'In hindsight it was a superficial approach to culture rather than a forensic test.' MANAGING PARTNER LONDON LAW FIRM

Cultural differences were highlighted in how decisions were communicated to staff. We were told that the autocratic style of one firm meant that they did not engage with their staff, which caused resentment, which in turn caused morale issues. The other firm had a more consultative approach: staff were kept informed and knew that at each stage they were apprised of what was happening and the process was transparent.

'Culture is key for all. Egos on legs do not work for us. Of course, all decent lawyers have a bit of an ego, but we have a strict 'no dickhead' policy, we like nice people.' MANAGING PARTNER REGIONAL LAW FIRM

An acquisitive firm told us that their culture attracted a firm that had already had an approach from two other firms.

'It was important to them that we did not get rid of staff as soon as we had merged, and we could reassure them that that was not our style. We knew that as a larger firm our procedures and processes to help best practice would be very different to theirs, and it would take a while for them to get up to speed, so we were open and honest about it. We created an environment that would help them succeed if we merged. We got them to talk to staff and partners from an earlier acquisition we had gone

through, they could ask any questions on anything where they had doubt, and in that process, they knew that what we said was what we did.'
CEO REGIONAL LAW FIRM

Can you recognise your leadership style, because of course it varies? Is it dictatorial or consultative, clear, or diffuse? Do you promote rigid processes and consistency or do you have a more adaptable and open style? Collaborative leaders advocate for change and empower their teams and encourage confidence and top-down decision making. You may prefer structure and precise style to make your teams more efficient with a distinct hierarchy. Do you empower your team or control them? To align cultures, you need to recognise the cultural differences that you have. That will enable you to take the best from both firms. A shift in style can lead to a loss of staff who do not like change. If you lose top talent, it will undermine value in the integration when your intellectual capital is drained.

What about your ability to change? Are you willing to risk new things, or will you always maintain the current state? If you are unwilling to work through the inevitable difficulties in creating a new firm, and implement new strategies, it will not work. How do your people work together? Is your structure formal and defined or more informal? Merged firms must interface between functions. If those interfaces are inconsistent, processes break down and employees on both sides will become frustrated and will fail to see why the other side cannot understand how work in their eyes should be done. What are your beliefs regarding success? Do you have a focus on your 'star players' or on teamwork? This can lead to a breakdown in getting work done. If a team must integrate star players whose notion of success is individual performance, then the team will feel a lack of support for getting the job done.

What assumptions were made and, with hindsight, what was learned?

It is not an easy task to overcome cultural differences. If you try and impose new cultural values on people by telling them what they are, it will be unlikely that it will replace their underlying values and beliefs held long-term in their current firm. Whilst there are different types of culture in each firm, they can be changed. Culture starts at the top of the firm and management must be able to articulate what the ethos is, or they will be unable to define it to their teams to help them contribute to the behaviours you want to see promoted in your culture. All staff, from the managing partner to the most junior member of staff, should know what the firm's culture is and how they contribute to it.

'Whilst culture is important it can be different, as long as there is an underlying purpose and vision that is very important.'
MANAGING PARTNER LONDON LAW FIRM

Dig deep and determine what is important to each firm because, once you have that, you are able to define what it is you would like to happen culturally, the cultural vision for the firm and the guiding principles which will help you define a strong culture. Individual personalities affect cultural values; not every leadership style suits everyone. Cultural styles can appear to be aligned because no one has done anything more than a superficial foray into cultural styles. However, unless there is alignment there will be a significant impact on decision making and leadership style. Recognise the differences and stop culture from undermining the desired goals of the merger.

'Never let culture provide an excuse for putting up with poor performance or resisting change.' MANAGING PARTNER LONDON LAW FIRM

There will be misconceptions about both firms and their cultural styles. It may have come from stories in the press that people believe, or anecdotes heard in the market and born out of gossip, but they are just that – stories which are not based on facts. Use positive factual stories to overcome these alleged facts.

'Culture is like family. Every family has a patriarch or matriarch who is the senior figure the family listen to. Like all families they fight and argue amongst themselves, but it gets sorted out. The trouble happens if an outsider takes issue with one of your family, it is acceptable for you to argue but is not tolerated from an outsider.'
PRAGNESH MODHWADIA, MANAGING PARTNER AXIOM DWFM

Focus on business value so people buy into your cultural vision and support it, because as long as there is an underlying purpose and vision, cultural differences can be dealt with, and you will be able to stop any detrimental culture from undermining your desired goals. You can give the newly merged firms a vision of the new culture and encourage behaviours so the best of the culture of both firms is enhanced, because there is a real chance to create a desired culture in a newly merged firm. Above all, remember – firms do not transform, people do.

'Culture is important, and if it doesn't align there is a real struggle. You have to be aware that if you are acquiring a smaller firm that they will tell you what you want to hear because they need to merge to survive.'
MANAGING PARTNER REGIONAL LAW FIRM

If you have a cultural strategy, you can be specific about your culture to stand out in the market. If you want to win awards as an innovative firm, encourage innovators by recognising ideas. You will always add value across the firm if you understand your culture. Explaining cultural change is not enough. Staff need to know why it is necessary, and open communication will help them accept change and stop them feeling that everything they have known is under threat. Do not be frightened to reassess and re-evaluate your original cultural integration strategy, because things can and do change.

'We always wanted to keep our culture because people like working for us. We want them to enjoy coming to work but still be commercial. We want people to really feel part of something.'
MANAGING PARTNER SE REGIONAL LAW FIRM

It takes a concerted effort to understand culture and it needs to come from the top, because culture affects everyone. To gain a new culture you must understand the culture both firms have pre-merger, then determine what it is you do well and what it is that you want to do better. To get culture right you must be very clear about the behaviours you want to promote and reinforce, and that will strengthen the new entity. Once you have defined them you can look at how you can practically encourage and promote them. Use accountable and relatable management leaders throughout the firm to help promote the new culture. This can be as simple as respecting how everyone's time is equally important, so meetings could have a different approach, with all invited parties ensuring that they are available. Have an agenda and give everyone the opportunity to contribute, rather than one dominant individual powering through decisions that they want and others finding an excuse not to attend because they know that that they will be strong-armed into decisions they do not agree with, but where they have no opportunity to debate what it is they do want.

'Quite often culture reflects the personalities of the partners.'
MANAGING PARTNER SW LAW FIRM

One of the reasons we heard integration was sought was to gain high-level staff and to offer them a defined career path, and to ensure that highly valued staff were retained within the firm. The firm's culture gives a sense of identity that staff recognise, are proud of and want to be part of. From a firm's perspective you should strive for excellence not only in your approach to clients, but it should extend to your responsibilities to your employees, who recognise that excellence in everything you do.

'No wonder there was a continuous stream of people fighting to leave. We had backstabbing associates, warring partners, downtrodden PAs and two directors for every business operation function, all jockeying for position. When the problem starts at the top the solution should start there to fix it, and that's exactly where we started.' CEO LONDON LAW FIRM

A merger team can help you cascade your new cultural messages by identifying and using the best influencers within the firm. Decide which behaviours and practices you want to promote in your new culture and design a set of desirable cultural attributes, which are customer-focussed, innovative, decisive, team-oriented and respectful to others. Once defined you can look for practical ways to encourage and then promote them. Firms with a strong corporate culture thrive, so culture and its alignment should be key to any M&A integration.

Culture is a powerful tool, which used well helps people thrive when fully aligned to your business strategy, and will support the business goals you envisioned with the merger or acquisition.

'**If we had measured the culture, we would never have gone ahead. We made it work.**' CEO TOP 100 LAW FIRM

Case study
We have first-hand experience of working with two firms who both said they had a collegiate culture. The reality was very different because their decision-making style was fundamentally different. One was, in fact, very collegiate, so no decisions were made and the other was a benevolent dictatorship, so the merger integration was not working. We had to work with them to identify a set of objectives and a vision for the new firm to buy into.
CEO TOP 100 LAW FIRM

Case study
We spoke to a firm whilst culturally aligned in many areas they had a different style in how operations staff were viewed. One firm were consultative, the other hierarchical. Quite literally, we will consult with our staff and seek opinion versus get on and do as you have been asked. Recognising that difference gave them a base to build from and stopped potential frustrations from boiling over and becoming 'You would say that you are from X firm.' The recognition was that both firms knew that they must recognise an environment where debate was needed without staff feeling that they had been talked over or shouted down, when in fact their contribution was worthwhile.
MANAGING PARTNER REGIONAL LAW FIRM

CHAPTER 4

Do partners help or hinder mergers?

'In a room partners would vote for whatever was being asked but would go out and behave differently in their own office, which caused friction.'
MANAGING PARTNER REGIONAL LAW FIRM

The business of lawyers is to advise others, but it is a very different issue to make key decisions about their own business, which they are not used to. There are numerous studies that highlight why mergers fail. The reality is that the number of challenges are pervasive and must be faced throughout the process and partners and lawyers are front and centre of those challenges. At the start of a merger the excitement is tangible and everyone looks at changes that will have a better outcome for everyone involved. For every partner it is a personal journey. If they are accustomed to having authority and must vote for something that may remove that authority it is a huge decision. Whilst partners may find the prospect of a merger exciting, the reality can be very different, however willing they might be in theory. How you secure partner buy-in will come down to how you champion the vision and benefits of the combined firms from the beginning of potential merger or acquisition talks. Their expectations need careful management, and this starts at the onset of those discussions.

'There are so many complexities and difficulties when you are merging that you get drawn down into the detail; having a joint vision is paramount but people get into the weeds and fallout.'
MANAGING PARTNER REGIONAL LAW FIRM

Partners essentially own individual businesses in their practice areas which combine to make the firm as a whole. Why would partners support or seek to undermine or block a merger? There are several groups in a merger that should be considered. The first is obviously those who support it. Some partners are visionary and will see clear benefits of a merger; they will want to enhance their earnings, with improved profitability, gain security, better prospects and attract clients that may not have considered working with the smaller entity, so they now have the ability to enter new markets. They will see how merging teams will enable succession planning with a pool of dynamic staff. For some it will in time enable them to leave and have a guarantee of getting their equity out of the firm.

How partners are paid can significantly impact their behaviour. If you encourage a silo mentality and 'eat what you kill' culture you will inhibit teamwork. Ideally you will have a range of criteria that help determine compensation with soft skills that have a positive impact. What measures do you take to deal with and protect the firm against dissenting partners, and are they easy to spot? We need to consider those who are fearful. For many the very mention of merger and acquisition will bring fear and uncertainty. How will new profit-sharing arrangements affect them, will they maintain their clients, will they lose authority when decision-making structures change?

'Lawyers are a pessimistic bunch who look for the worst in everything. It's their training, so they will definitely look for the worse in any merger or acquisition.' MANAGING PARTNER LONDON LAW FIRM

Will they now vie with their new colleagues for key positions in the new structure and have to jostle to maintain their practice areas and key client relationships? What will happen to colleagues they have always worked with and the allies that have supported them? If they have never been expected to work to targets and they are introduced, they are being asked to make significant adjustments. They may perceive that they will never be appreciated in the same way that they are used to. Are they in fact going to lose everything that they are familiar with? In all likelihood there will be a new LLP agreement, and what are the implications of that? Will it be more restrictive so they will be unable to walk away if they do not like the merger? They may not be encouraged that business and cultural issues will be resolved and realigned, and they may know that they will face an involuntary exit and have to start again elsewhere.

In all this change people are unsettled, so how do you ensure that partners will actually vote for a merger? To do that you must articulate clearly right from the outset the potential benefits that merger or acquisition will bring, with a vision of success that they will buy into. You must put a strong case before them and ensure that you debate every aspect. If you do not, partners may appear to support you and do the absolute opposite. Do not bury difficult issues – inevitably you will have to have challenging conversations and be clear and open about what is happening. Share your vision and continually return to it or you will have a group of agnostics whose hearts and minds have not been won and who will cause issues as you move forward. You can protect the firm from dissenting partners by ensuring that they know what it is they are voting for with the merger. This takes an investment in time, clear and careful planning, and support, because if you do not you will have people tell you it is not what they voted for.

'I had the awkward squad, two-three senior partners that turned against the merger from the beginning, using anything as a reason not to move forward with the merger. They had the most to lose financially from the merger as they were all due to retire within the next two years, so they put their individual needs ahead of the firm, they then took more junior partners along with them and the merger stalled.'
MANAGING PARTNER REGIONAL LAW FIRM

What about those who want to maintain everything as it is, a safe option and maintain the status quo, harmless because it is perceived that they are easily won over, not vehement either way? This is a powerful group in a firm because they fear change and 'rash moves', and can cause inertia, which will stall out a merger. Of course, and unavoidably will be the anti-group. However, there is a perception that this group will be anti a merger just to be difficult, and they in fact may feel threatened by any merger, but there may be a range of reasons. Through their own connections do they believe that they have identified what is a better merger option. The reality is that their forays into that option were probably peripheral, lacking any real analysis, but it was their idea, they know people in that firm and that can be hard to let go of. They may believe that the suggested merger partner will not actually deliver all the benefits you have highlighted for moving forward with this choice of firm, so the case for the merger has not been made strongly enough. Perhaps they feel especially threatened by this particular merger. They may support the proposal if you present coherent reasons for it. However, they may obstinately block it unless they get something they want rather than accepting that you are looking to benefit the firm as a whole, not the individuals vehemently opposed to it. They are an extreme group of individuals who will use it as a power play to either gain favourable terms for themselves or to leave.

There will be vigorous debate amongst partners during any merger discussions as pros and cons are deliberated; there might well be fragmentation in the partnership that changes as arguments are made and pondered. It is an emotional time which can lead to real fragmentation as things are said in the heat of the moment that can never be 'unsaid' and which disrupt the harmony of the firm. Partners can and do behave in ways that are easily picked up on by the rest of the firm, and this is where rumour control can get out of hand, especially where an increase in meetings is taking place behind closed doors and supposition becomes fact for some. The impact of poor behaviour can have a detrimental effect not only on disgruntled partners but on the rest of the firm who pick up on their demeanour. It can impact performance as people become distracted by the merger and lose sight of the necessity to carry on business as usual. Partners can become very defensive about their own role, especially if they fear loss of power, and without realising it become assertive to the point of aggression and power play to assert their place.

Whilst all of this is happening there is a real danger of leaking the intention of a merger externally, inadvertently or deliberately, and if it is deliberate, it will be done to promote a point of view partners want aired.

Behavioural issues will impact when partners from both firms meet to discuss the merger, and these behaviours are usually well hidden and therefore more shocking when they come in to play. Partners may be rude, surly or just refuse to engage with their counterparts in the other firm. Meetings become superficial 'chats' where everyone plays nicely but no issues are properly debated in any depth and they walk away with every reason not to proceed. More dangerous is that it is seen as nothing major, and the merger goes ahead. How do these behavioural issues emerge once the deal has been done? Time and again during our research we heard of firms where the merger deal becomes all-consuming and deal euphoria sets in because it has been an intense period taking many months to come to fruition, and everyone is exhausted. Integration now becomes the real issue. Those who were visionary about the merger will try and push forward all the integration issues because they will want to see the benefits as soon as possible. Integration always throws up issues and those who did not want to move forward, even though they said they did and voted in favour, will seize upon these issues and proclaim it is not working. They will see this as an opportunity to undermine everything, including the leadership, and they will happily discuss this externally as well as internally. Those who were in that 'safe group' can easily be head-hunted away because the status quo they wanted to keep has now been challenged and eroded.

If leaders have not prepared for this, perhaps they decided not to employ a strong project leader, they now face dealing with these issues whilst trying to carry on with business as usual. At this point of exhaustion, when the euphoria of the deal has dissipated, they deny that there are any behavioural issues because it is easier to ignore them than deal with them. All those issues will come to the fore, 'I knew it wouldn't work', 'Our IT systems were always better and now the new system doesn't work.'

If fissures become fractures, then the market hears about it, and it becomes easy to pick off star players and teams and move them out of the business. The value of any potential merger is dissipated to the degree it stalls out. To avoid this, you should actively target partners that you want to stay by ensuring they really do understand the proposition and benefits of the merger, and by listening to any concerns they may have; it will be time well invested.

'Differences were worked through because partners were loyal to the overall vision of the merger.' MANAGING PARTNER LONDON LAW FIRM

You need to be a visionary leader from the start to stop this happening, because if it does it will affect the entire firm. Your project director will stop you being drawn down into the minute detail that stalls merger integration. You need your partners to be positive advocates who have a shared and deep understanding of the benefits of the two firms coming together and can promote those throughout the firm.

Issues that became contentious and part of the ammunition of the 'I didn't vote for that' team, because they were not clearly and fully debated, included:

Hidden costs

Have you ensured that your partners fully understand the costs of your potential merger or acquisition? Few firms actually explore what those costs might be; they hint at them or obfuscate about them. If you underestimate costs, partners who may have appeared to be on side and then see a dilution of profits will be disruptive, especially if they believe that those costs have not been fully debated. You can assess costs at the same time you look at valuation and due diligence. Use professionals to help you develop that cost estimate, which will include areas such as technology, marketing, branding and PR. Ensure that the costs of the merger do not outweigh the benefits.If you do this early on it will help you identify potential issues and problems, and it will aid your decision-making processes because it has become transparent, and it will show clearly how both parties approach it.

Technology

Technology costs must be considered, ever more so in the aftermath of the pandemic when we have had a greater reliance on IT with remote working, which looks set to continue. The combined firm will move to one platform, and quite often one firm will have already invested more in that area. Your project team will be able to help you determine a realistic costing that is fit for purpose in the new firm.

Property costs

You may be considering moving or just re-configuring you current building, but you still need an estimate.

PII costs

This cost was raised copious times in our research, where due diligence had been inadequate. Firms paid claims but did not claim through their insurance broker to hide the fact they were taking place, but those claims still had to be paid for. We heard of claims where one side was told the claim was in hand and minimal and in fact cost several million more than declared, which directly impacted PEP for several years.

Marketing, Business Development and PR

Your newly combined firm will need to invest in this area, yet it is the one area we see pushed aside in the hope of saving money. Have you considered how you are going to promote the new entity and differentiate your brand, cross-sell to ensure the new initiatives you told partners would be a benefit, and how this will actually develop?

Staff costs

A common thread in our study was the need to acquire higher quality professional operations staff needed for the size of the newly combined firm. Whilst those that went down this path told us what a huge difference it made, it comes at a cost. Partners must be made aware of this, rather than the illusion that you can produce the quality of staff required at the same cost as before.If you involve partners at an early stage of the discussions it is essential that you continually sell the benefits, or inertia will and does set in.

What assumptions were made and with hindsight what was learned?

Do not presume that because everyone voted for the merger or acquisition they are on side with every decision, or that once the deal is brokered everything else will fall into place. Partners will obfuscate by debating and getting entrenched in the smallest aspects and not letting go, to the extent that they will not consider the bigger picture. Show people the reason for the merger and do not let lawyers get involved in the detail because they will argue about the detail, not the principle. This is the prefect reason to have a project director on board with a team that have the authority to act, because merger or acquisition is not a time for consensus when decisions must be made. To get partners to vote on everything is not feasible in a merger. A dedicated Project Director with the authority to act is essential. Managing Partners of the merging firms need to have a joint vision and purpose from day one. Your project team will approach each issue that arises as a team. They will not be adversarial, they will understand what partner approval looks like, but it is not essential that everyone is one hundred percent on board. Really listen to the issues that your partners bring up at the start of the process and ensure that you deal with them. Discuss billable time targets, profit and margin targets early on to avoid future major conflicts. If you do not deal with their issues they can stir up full insurrection amongst other partners who were on side. Be aware, however, of offering too many concessions to partners who are making things difficult, because it may result in some of the commercial benefits of the merger being diluted. If you believe that they are deadwood and they were on your list to deal with after the merger this could be the ideal opportunity to part company with them, especially if they are unprofitable.

'We worked hard to ensure partners bought into the vision of the new firm. We lobbied powerful partners to help bring others in line.'
CEO LONDON LAW FIRM

Show partners what it is you want to achieve with the merger. The merger will only be successful and deliver the expected benefits if sufficient partners in the merged firm combine to help deliver the benefits and proactively support the achievement of client synergies, business development, operational enhancement, cost savings and the adoption of new systems and processes. You need transparency over everything in a merger or acquisition to avoid 'them and us' issues.

'We were helped because we had robust processes in place, and it becomes hard for partners to reject a process if it was logical, fair and had been voted for by them.' CEO LONDON LAW FIRM

Although lawyers love words, if they have not bought into the reasons for the merger or acquisition it is not sufficient to give partners a pack of information with the expectation that they will read it fully and agree with it. It is essential that at every stage it is weighed up, considered, contested and debated as necessary. Put in effort early to stop people being disgruntled. You must have clarity and inclusiveness. Power players can de-rail the process if they feel they are being treated poorly.

'Only one in ten partners had actually read the detailed prospectus we put together.' COO TOP 100 LONDON LAW FIRM

'We made sure that both parties shared a monthly information pack. At meetings we discussed that pack. It was only after a year of those in-depth discussions that we decided to move forward. We had a layered approach, one step at a time. It really worked because at every meeting both sides

learned more and we had open discussions.'
COO TOP 100 LONDON LAW FIRM

If you have partners who constantly try and hold up the merger, are they acting in the best interests of the firm, when you have shared the benefits with them of what the merger can achieve? Remind partners of their duty to the partnership above their personal interests. Give them a vision of what the new firm would look like and facilitate it with meetings and workshops.

'If we believe that our partners are straying, we bring them back on course and remind them that they agreed to the plan, and why they agreed.'
MANAGING PARTNER LONDON LAW FIRM

If partners decide to disrupt the merger integration once the deal has been signed, what did they not believe and why did they not trust you? You did not convince them that the merged firm would be better than the two individual entities. To keep the partners and teams you want in the newly created firm is constant hard work. Partners need to see fair and proportionate change and they will agree to whatever is being asked of them and then walk out and sabotage the deal if their concerns have not been met. If one side continually refers to you as 'that lot', they have not been shown the value of the merger and what it could mean to them, so they have no sense of unity. Partners will get involved in the detail if you let them, and chip away at small things, because major change is so daunting. This will stall out a merger.

Partners are often concerned about everything they will have to give up, including their autonomy and being less involved in decisions that affect the firm, but the reality is that in a new firm some partners will have to cede control; that has to be debated and not hidden

'We reassured partners throughout that it would be fair. We said that they had to take a leap of faith. Why would we want them to be disgruntled?
MANAGING PARTNER REGIONAL LAW FIRM

Case study
We spoke to a firm where a senior team member blocked everything that they perceived would change things they had known and worked with, even though

they would benefit the new entity.

'We had one senior blocker, everything that was positive in terms of change they railed against: we compromised so often but in the end we had no choice but to part company with them to move forward in the way that we had envisioned.' MANAGING PARTNER LONDON AND REGIONAL LAW FIRM

Another participant told us that they are a limited company rather than a partnership. They anticipate that where partners are used to having a say in all decisions, that doesn't happen in a limited company where the MD makes the decisions and what they say happens. There is simply no consensus by committee. Profitability is then not a driver because joining partners move straight to a salary as a director and everyone is at the same level of salary. A partner title, often a hang-up for people, is irrelevant in a limited company.

One participating firm told us that they have one question that they always ask first. 'What are your expectations?' If this is not sorted out things can quickly get muddled, and it must be addressed.

'We had an early exchange of accounts and ours were better so there was already an inequality. You do not want to appear pompous so I rang the Managing Partner and said, 'My partners earn X and yours Y, we cannot join you as it will water down profits per partner for us and my partners will say no. If you have an interest in merging with us tell me what your expectations are.' It is a difficult conversation to have. Profit per partner has to match – there is no other way. You can compromise on other things, but if they are looking for a premium it is not for us.' STEVE BULMAN MANAGING PARTNER WBW SOLICITORS INCORPORATING BEVISS & BECKINGSALE

'We wanted to know what partner approval looked like and did it have to have one hundred percent everyone on board. Our negotiating team approached each issue as a team and did not have an adversarial approach. We had so many partner groups they approached them collectively. Both firms shared a deep understanding of why we were coming together and we had a real axis of trust and as leaders we emphasised that.' MANAGING PARTNER REGIONAL LAW FIRM

CHAPTER 5

2+2 does not always equal 4 and you may not want it to

As the headline to this chapter suggests, the assessment as to what any merged or combination of practices may look like is certainly not as simple as just adding together the most recent profit and loss accounts of each one and assuming that will be the combined practice.

As you can imagine, this is not only dangerous, short-sighted and naïve from both sides, but also very lazy from whichever side is leading the transaction.

Any combination should not be looked at simply as that sum of 2 + 2 equalling 4, but as a fully explained analysis of the benefits that it will bring by that additional expertise, geographical reach or simply more collaborative opportunities, which hopefully will drive revenue higher than purely that combined, sum of the parts figure I just referred to.

It is very important to be clear with both sides / firms within the merger equation, especially where all parties are going to be invested financially in the enlarged firm, what success will look like from a financial perspective going forward.

There can also be an unhealthy interest in saving costs. This may well be true in the fact that you will only need one finance head and, sadly, some of that team may be surplus to requirements, and perhaps professional indemnity insurance premiums will be lower (more about that later). The cost-saving fixation should not in my view be the main focus, certainly at initial stages of assessment. Look for the plusses and then further analysis and due diligence ('DD'), which is so important, can have a more wide-ranging and detailed review.

Readers of this chapter may well think it is a strange thing for an accountant to say that you should not simply believe the figures that are in front of you, that these should need reviewing in more detail as, surely, they have been prepared by an accountant after all?! Delving deeper into the figures is key to identifying risks that you did not initially think may be there. To get a true picture of what sits behind the headline numbers should ensure that ultimately the decision to press ahead and combine the two entities is correct for all.

So, what could be worth looking at in more detail?

Income recognition

The earn-out element and value of related Work In Progress (WIP) methodology should be agreed early otherwise that can be a source of discontent and massive issues between parties at a later date.

An example of this comes from one of my fellow Menzies partners, DD specialist Ross Wiggins. During a recent assignment the relevance of income recognition came to light via a change in Work In Progress (WIP valuation methodology of one practice from accounting period to accounting period. The basis was frankly never consistent and perhaps was not being done to provide a true reflection of results. This is a lesson that not every WIP (or amounts recoverable on contracts) methodology is the same. This may not just affect historical analytical comparisons but also any earn-out. As what (ever-changing) WIP valuation would be right to use then? This is not necessarily about recoverability rates but perhaps finding a consistent, agreed approach to valuing the WIP that does not skew comparisons between the two firms, and enables us to make profit and cashflow projections going forward that are not either meaningless or impossible / deluded.

Covid effects

There are certainly matters that can be very relevant to merger discussions that have come to light, or rather come more into focus, because of the pandemic, and I will now look at a couple of these and how they ought to be viewed during any merger courting.

IT and WFH

A firm's IT infrastructure, IT internal set-up and reporting within the management structure, along with simply the age of the kit as at April 2020, was a good indication as to how the firm would cope during the pandemic, and how the firm can now cope in respect of remote and flexible working going forward. Those lawyers who simply decided they were key workers and therefore had to still work in the office were quite possibly within firms, or perhaps even managing firms, that did not have the infrastructure to facilitate that remote homeworking which was part of the way of stopping the spread of coronavirus. The point here is that this may well tell any acquiring firm exactly how much investment they need to make immediately in computers, networking and infrastructure generally to match their own, and to bring their new colleagues up to that level where working from home is exactly the same as in the office from a connectivity and reliability perspective.

In my experience, this lack of previous investment has caused valuations to be aggressively chipped and conversations around the value of computer equipment to become quite 'pointed' as regard shortcomings that are believed to exist in IT.

Staff – your key asset

Staff are obviously any firm's key asset and, not unconnected to the previous point as regards to flexible working, is how staff have been treated during the pandemic. Have they been forced to come into the office when they would rather not? To any business combination this could be viewed as a positive if the reputation of the acquiring firm is one that has that sought-after flexibility and can retain and attract staff. The opposite would be, though, if the first interaction of colleagues is that the acquiring firm is perhaps not as good as they thought they were in respect of staff empathy and communication during the pandemic, with perhaps a number looking to walk in any case.

In the legal sector, like many, where recruiting and retaining is crucial, it might be useful for both firms to either conduct or share survey results to understand any gaps that their staff may believe there are in both aspects, as a good place to start to see if there are inherent problems already which could well affect the success of the combined entity. Whilst not an approach often recommended, that transparency once staff are 'in the know' can be hugely appreciated by all staff.

Culture – does it come through in the numbers?

Many people talk about the culture of any business and the fact that this can be assessed almost from the time they walk in the building, but this is not always the case as over the last 21 months the return of a receptionist from a long furlough stint can go one of two ways. Whilst that person may be resentful and perhaps not the buoyant and dynamic face that you would wish your clients and contacts to see immediately on entering the building, the reverse could be true, and they are very grateful to have the job retained and therefore a shining light as anyone first enters the building. The opposite may be true of the firm's engine room that has worked far too long hours throughout the pandemic, coupled with the stamp duty holiday and the effects on the conveyancing teams that may have gone unrecognised in some firms.

So again, be careful of what seems a motivated team simply from the productivity figures and perhaps even improved profitability on those previous year ends: this can be masking underlying issues.

Clients – quite important also

Also key, is a review of client type or client concentration risk, as Ross Wiggins describes it. Additionally, what are the average fee levels, charge-out rates, pricing structures and internal policies, as there will often need to be an alignment which may lead to churn, which would undoubtedly be unwelcome. Don't also forget any conflicts within both client bases that could immediately eliminate turnover.

These are all important issues to feed into projections and try and eliminate those unwanted surprises post deal. After all, that is the benefit of the hindsight we are trying to achieve.

Covid spike – some revenues up, some expenditure down

That rather conveniently brings me to another issue in respect of DD at the moment, given that results in many firms have shown a spike, especially in certain teams as referred to above – particularly conveyancing – and how these can possibly mislead those tasked with financial DD and also those putting together projections as to where they see fee levels in the near- and medium-term future.

There is general acceptance that much of the expenditure has stalled over recent time, for example networking and travel (especially international where international networks exist); this also includes partners and staff in firms travelling between offices where virtual meeting rooms have rather proved that it was not actually necessary before. It is these costs coming back on stream, the timing and to what degree, that makes it very difficult plugging into those projections going forward. This is not just tricky in respect of your own firm but even more difficult if you are assessing that of a firm where you do not have that intimacy of knowledge, and whether any of that travelling / networking produced a sensible ROI that you would actually want it to recommence in any case?

Professional indemnity

It has generally been accepted that the professional indemnity market has been challenging for a few years now.

Firms on both sides of the merger equation should not lose sight of the fact that the historical assumption that the combined entities' professional indemnity insurance will go down, whilst still not unreasonable, should not be assumed as a certainty, especially given that in some cases a 20% to 30% increase in premiums exists in any case.

The combined entities' split of fees will also affect the attractiveness of the PI market to a firm, and this is incredibly focussed at present on the conveyancing market and percentage of that type of work to the overall revenue of the firm.

Very early discussions with brokers on both sides is encouraged, and the dominant party in the discussions should not simply assume that their broker or their insurer can get the best deal. I have seen discussions that have flipped and it is the broker's insurance company of the smaller player which has ultimately provided the much better solution. This is another indication that previously generally accepted assumptions do not simply play out in modern-day merger and acquisition activity.

It is also not simply a case of looking at claims history, previous premiums and make an assumption and moving forward, that is a very dangerous game to play.

Again, you should delve deeper into the figures and look at perhaps the number of possible claims which have been paid away to clients as to an indication that perhaps there is more risk within the practice than is simply suggested from the premiums paid.

A complete review of the complaints procedures and associated records would also give a good indication of the level, trends, and specific work types where there appears to be more risk than others. Linked to this would be a large number of debtor balances or unbilled WIP outstanding, which can indicate that service is not at the optimum level and therefore clients are either not paying as they are not happy, or that fee earners are not confident enough to bill work in progress as they believe themselves that service levels have not been up to the standard. This can also indicate not just issues potentially arising with professional indemnity, but also a practice that is not overly attractive to acquire.

Goodwill – still relevant?

For a while now there have been many commentators saying that no cheques are being written in respect of goodwill for practices being purchased. I can happily say that this is not the case and there are practices that are being marketed and have completed to a deal that are worthy of goodwill payment on a trade and assets purchase. This has happened and it is not just consolidators who can structure a deal to achieve a goodwill payment.

I do agree that the deal has to be structured correctly to ensure that full value for that goodwill being paid does pass across for the enduring benefit of the equity partners / owners in the purchasing firm. Perhaps I should say, the enduring benefit of the practice making the acquisition, as often some of these deals fall over because senior equity partners within acquiring firms do not see a benefit to themselves in the short term. Those same people seem to, for that moment, lose sight of / forget their custodian ethos, and perhaps just view that this is not in their best interests, rather than actually being in the practice's long-term best interests.

Structure of any deal

This is probably the area of negotiation that as advisers we simply have to suggest that the price is purely the meeting point of a willing buyer and a willing seller. For both parties that can depend upon the structure proposed. It can, as with goodwill these days, not simply be a mathematical formula although obviously useful as a guide.

Often for the seller there is a bias towards a goodwill payment as this can be much more attractive to them for tax reasons, but the reverse is often the case for the purchaser.

This is especially true where the purchaser is an LLP or partnership/sole trader, as any relief for goodwill payment will only be available on the ultimate sale of their practice, so not ideal at that moment in time.

The adage that the tax tail should not wag the commercial dog is also very apt here, in the scenario that both parties should be looking beyond tax efficiency and try and ensure that whatever deal they are putting together focuses on the resulting combination, especially where all parties are looking to continue in business together.

A combination where one party or parties is/are looking to retire shortly after will obviously skew discussions, and often migrates to whether a goodwill valuation is still appropriate where professional indemnity run-off is being avoided in a successor practice scenario.

It is getting these possible variations or negotiation stances in to focus early so that they can be ironed out at an early stage. If you are too far apart at the start, then either one party needs educating on the value actually there or the other needs to lose the deluded stance. Getting this sorted early saves a lot of time or simply highlights that the deal is not possible and everybody moves on.

One danger in this negotiation process is that it should not be an ego trip for one party, as I have seen cases where it is all about getting a deal, any deal. This will only lead to a disaster at some point and again this is where third party advisers prove their worth in ensuring firms do not go down that route.

The initial information exchanges

Whether you decide to be the predator or the prey you will be required to exchange various information, and generally this would cover the following:

1. Three years' PII applications and cover details. In my experience this is often the first initial request. You do not want to be taking on

other people's problems, and certainly this request can save wasted time on both sides. I have been involved in discussions that end at this point, saying 'Come back in two years once you've sorted your claims record out';

2. Three years' accounts, but do appreciate that further break-down and drill-down may well be (and should be) requested;

3. Lease details;

4. Significant recent leavers and joiners and any planned upcoming recruitment. This is never a bad thing to do in any case, as it links in nicely with departments' capacities and the firm's overall production capacity vs. turnover budgets as discussed elsewhere;

5. Partner demographics – age profile;

6. Next generation – bright young things;

7. Client analysis – top 10/20 per department; 2-page Information Memorandum (IM);

8. Drafted Non-Disclosure Agreement (NDA);

9. Drafted questionnaire for the other side.

Whether you are the deemed buyer or seller, it pays to be DD ready, so the above is something that you should ensure is available before you commence on this journey – in fact for a practice that takes its own strategy seriously, most of this should already be to hand.

Using a broker often in combination with your own accountant or other Trust Adviser is quite effective You have someone you have worked with for a long time who understands the way you work, and the external broker tasked with obtaining and sourcing the right targets It enables you to concentrate on the day job and is often much more cost-effective as fee structures can be flexible. It can also very much assist the confidentiality and, as an example, the broker may know someone who meets your criteria, which takes everyone neatly to the next stage. It is also worthwhile appointing a negotiating team which would report back on progress to the rest of the partnership at key points, which again ensures everyone else can crack on with their day job.

So bearing these points in mind, you have a list you are comfortable with to move to the next stage. This would undoubtedly be a point in time where the appointed negotiating team would report back on progress to the rest of the partnership. This maintains focus, assists confidentiality and, where DD is being carried out, ensures reporting lines with external advisers are clear.

Sensitivity analysis, projections going forward

Crucial, and not just useful for DD but as your initial roadmap for the enlarged practice. You will want to see how you are immediately mapping against those projections to assess how the merger is likely to progress, and then in real-time whether this is being achieved? Now a great focus for a partner group is how much free cash there is, or headroom in the projections once any debt finance has been exhausted, and that additional finance that may be required is only coming from one place, the partner group.

In summary and hindsight

The trick, as Anne suggests throughout the book, is to take advantage of hindsight as much as possible, covering all aspects. As regards the financials this would be:

- In advance: difficult, you may say, as that is not really what hindsight is all about, but put yourselves through excellent research, analysis, market knowledge and that all-important DD in a position to have confidence in how your combined future will pan out.

- After the deal: track the projections and analysis, trends of activity and productivity to get early sight of any issues that could impact on what you hope the success of the combined entity will look like. And always have your vision of what success looks like.

CHAPTER 6

Financial culture, the bedrock of a successful merger

For some time, succession planning has been a growing problem for legal practices. With an increasing age profile within law firm leaders and a lack of interest from prospective equity partners to take the helm, a merger seems a sensible solution.

The decision to merge with another legal practice provides an exceptional opportunity for both sides of the deal. An opportunity exists for the buyer to grow their business, which should bring together synergies within the types of work offered by the enlarged practice, creating more opportunities for others within the firm to progress their career.

For the seller, the merger gives an opportunity for ageing owners to leave the profession without the need to pay the astronomical costs associated with professional indemnity insurance run-off cover.

For both, a merger gives an opportunity to safeguard the interest of clients and an opportunity to continue offering trusted advice to some of the most vulnerable people in society.

Whatever the reasons behind the merger, once the departing owners have made the decision to merge, the people left in the business must have a voice. Success or failure of the new entity will depend on winning the hearts and minds of the entire workforce. Therefore, a plan to seamlessly integrate both sides of the merger is key to developing the culture of the business and for the buyer to ensure the merged practice delivers against its obligations.

Finance is rarely about the money

Discussions around finance can often be an emotive and sensitive topic. The financial consideration will undoubtedly play a part for both parties. They will each want to receive the best possible deal.

As each party will have their own personal reasons for completing the merger, it is critical to align expectations from the very start if the merger has any realistic chance of going ahead.

Aligning cultures

One aspect that is often omitted from conversation is the differences that will exist in both parties' cultural approach to business and, more specifically to this chapter, finance. It is here that the success of a merger can quickly be derailed so it is important to ensure the new merged entity (the NewCo) lives up to its expectations.

Unfortunately, we see repeated instances of mergers going horribly wrong, which will have serious repercussions for the equity stakeholders and the job satisfaction levels of employed staff. This can lead to valued staff leaving the business, which will undoubtably impact future fee income and create a barrier for the operational effectiveness of the business. Should this happen, the firm will struggle to meet the future earning potential outlined in the business plan/financial projections presented to the bank.

Knowing that to be the case, aligning financial cultures must be a priority exercise which is assigned to a senior leader in the business. From here on in, the thought process must be about the new enlarged company (the NewCo).

Find the right starting point

The SRA Code of Conduct for Firms (2.4) requires SRA registered legal practices to *actively monitor their financial stability and business viability*. Put simply, to satisfy the obligations of the management team, the appropriate level of financial due diligence should be completed. It is here you can evidence to all concerned that the merger has been properly considered. Why? Because all too often the merger can present future challenges because the due diligence has been lacking and where the future cash requirement has been misunderstood, causing the cashflow position to quickly dry up.

Funders will want to evidence the management capability to influence the future growth trajectory of the NewCo, and my personal view is that this cannot be truly evidenced without completing a few important tasks.

A pig wearing lipstick is still a pig

Two small, badly run practices coming together is likely to result in one large, badly run practice. Should any funding be required to support the merger, a lender will review the past performance of both businesses and base their decision to support the merger based on the management capability of the new entity.

The idea of Firm A being purchased, to allow exiting partners to sail into the sunset, may seem appealing, (for the departing partners at least) but for the rest of the staff they will want to avoid a disaster.

As an example: What should happen if the dominant merger partner has poor financial and operation controls and insists on steamrolling over the policies, controls and procedures which are deeply engrained within the merged practice?

Firm A (the seller) is a Lexcel Accredited legal practice. The firm is proud of their approach to financial and operational risk and has a culture of excellence which permeates through the firm. They have perfected their controls over many years and each member of staff has a consistent approach to financial and operational management.

On the other hand the buyer (Firm B) does not have the same level of controls and, as the more dominant player in the merger, insists Firm A adapts to their ways of working. Staff at firm A must now cope with the impending fallout of changing their entire policies, controls, and procedures to suit Firm B.

Needless to say, the new entity loses its Lexcel accreditation and the frustration in dealing with the differing approaches to financial and operational controls leads to animosity amongst the staff. In short, the cultural fit does not support the merger and key personnel leave the practice, which spells future disaster for the NewCo.

The lesson here is this: at an early stage it is crucial for the staff from both firms to spend time together understanding the controls used within each business. This can offer an opportunity to take the best from both firms to create a collegiate approach for the future.

Mark Twain commented, 'The secret of getting ahead is starting. The secret of getting started is breaking your tasks into smaller manageable tasks, and then starting on the first one.'

Thankfully there are a few free resources which are quick and easy to complete. The results should be used to support the due diligence process. The results will provide the new management team with a valuable insight on which to base their strategic financial and operational plans.

Financial stability scorecard

Assessing financial controls is an important element of the merger and both entities are advised to compare their respective approaches to the financial management of the business.

An effective way to analyse each respective approach is to complete a Financial Stability Scorecard exercise.

The Financial Stability Scorecard, offered by Gemstone Legal, (https://www.gemstonelegal.co.uk/financialstabilityscorecard) is the only one of its kind and is an essential resource to conduct a gap analysis on both firms' approach to financial management.

By completing 30 Yes/No-style multiple choice questions, the scorecard results will identify what the firm does well and where the business could improve its financial controls. The scorecard focuses on 3 important categories, which are Financial Management, Cash Management and Borrowing. The exercise takes less than 5 minutes.

The Financial Stability Scorecard drills into the approach of these 3 categories and offers immediate results, scored out of 50. Once the results are received, if the firm is left wondering how they can improve their score, and therefore their controls, the firm can request a comprehensive written report which is unique to the firm's responses.

Financial benchmarking

The second action which should be completed is a financial benchmarking exercise for each organisation. This exercise provides useful information which will allow the buyer to fully understand the performance of their acquisition target compared to industry-accepted performance metrics.

As part of their credit policy acceptance criteria, a bank will certainly measure the performance of both parties against industry metrics.

The Law Society Law Management Section, Nat West Bank and various specialist accountants will offer their own version of a financial benchmarking survey, so getting a copy of one of them should be relatively easy. By comparing results the buyer can gather a valuable insight into each firm's performance. It will also enable the buyer to provide useful supporting information to the bank.

When considering a merger, the importance of available cash is a key concern for all stakeholders. After all, cash is king and without it the business will not survive.

As an example, (taken from the Nat West Legal Report 2021):

A financial adviser might suggest a holding of 3 months' expenses as a target figure as this should cover most short-term emergencies, such as a period of unemployment or sickness. So, if a firm with fee income of £5 million has expenses of £3.6 million and makes a profit of £1.4 million, then the emergency cash fund or capacity in their facility with the bank needs to be £900,000.

The Nat West Survey reports that at the end of 2020, the average law firm held 11% of annual fees, which equated to 2 months' expenditure. (This includes inflated cash balances which have been borrowed via the government funding schemes)

Pre-pandemic (2019) firms reported they held only c1.5% of annual fees. This may be a crude comparison. However, you can see why many law firms would struggle to deal with an interruption to business leading to reduced cashflow.

The above might be a useful measure for firms to consider as they expand.

Help to benchmark the future combined entity

Banks will wish to understand the likely future performance of the merged entity before they agree to any funding proposals. Completing a financial benchmarking exercise to support cash flow projections is therefore crucial.

The Financial Benchmarking Scorecard offered by Gemstone Legal allows for projected performance figures of the new entity to be measured. As results are instantaneous the firm can easily measure and adjust the projected numbers to sense check financial projections. It is this evidence that will help the bank to consider the accuracy of the financial projections.

The scorecard can be found here: https://www.gemstonelegal.co.uk/financialbenchmarking.

Don't forget to include your cashier

Mergers can be disruptive and therefore law firm leaders will want to ensure a high level of discretion surrounds any conversations. It is, however, essential for the firm to consider anything in the business that will have an impact on finance. The obvious attention will focus on fee earners' metrics (time recording, billing and cash collection); however, every role within the business, from reception staff to managing partner/director, can have a positive impact on the financial performance of the business. I have listed 5 examples below.

Systems What cost is involved in merging systems and does the functionality on the chosen satisfy the data fields captured in the soon-to-be-dormant system? What is the cost for additional user licences?

Cross referrals What opportunities exist to cross refer the newly enlarged client base, and are staff confident and adequately trained to spot opportunities?

Difference in targets Is the thought process on targets aligned between senior leaders? How does this differ between organisations? What reporting packs are provided to fee earners and are they understood? What steps are taken to improve under-performance and what consideration is given to bonus payments?

Operation of client money Are the controls robust? Who should be the bank of choice for the future business? By comparing the Accountants Reports (AR1) are there issues to address (e.g. residual balances)?

Cost savings Compare the trial balance of both firms to understand business expenditure. What cost synergies can be made by both firms coming together? Are there contract terms which can be renegotiated?

The valuation

The task of valuing a legal practice is a complicated one and there is no 'one size fits all' formula.

As the cost of PI Insurance premiums has significantly increased, law firms will have the situation where the exiting partners are content to leave without having to pay run-off cover (which is 3 times the annual insurance premium). E.g. where a firm is paying £75k annual premium, the exiting partners would need to find £225k to complete an orderly wind-down of their business.

Often mergers valuations are based on net assets rather than a multiple of income or profits, as many firms do not have any tangible goodwill. Evidence suggests in many cases the exiting partners may feel satisfied to recover all or part of their initial invested capital and disregard any claim on goodwill.

Valuation examples may include

Net assets as a business value

When considering the net assets of the firm (assets less liabilities), it will be important to fully understand the granular details associated with the figures reported in the firm's balance sheet.

The figure can be easily misrepresented. For example, a law firm claiming to hold value in debtors which have remained outstanding for several years is highly unlikely to realise any payment from these clients and therefore lock-up values (DRs and WIP) must be properly tested.

Likewise a firm with deferred liabilities to HMRC (tax/VAT), or liable for the repayment of government funding (CBILS / Bounce back loans) can offer a misleading picture of the true level of cash available in the business.

Goodwill

If goodwill can be evidenced, then the valuation will normally reflect a book value based upon profit or fee income multiples. In this situation it would make sense for the partnership or members' agreement to outline how goodwill will be valued.

Average recurrent earnings

The other way of valuing a legal practice is to consider the average recurrent earnings and apply a multiple to it.

E.g. consider the last three years' average profit, EBITDA – earnings before interest, tax, depreciation and amortisation – and apply a weighting to the most recent figures and adjust for any one-off items including for partners' drawings/dividends.

If a two-partner practice is showing average profits of £200,000, however, each partner is paid £100,000, then that practice has not made any profit.

The multiple applied to the average earnings can vary depending on the type of work but can be up three times or more average retained earnings.

Facilitating the payment

Many mergers are now completed without any cash changing hands at the outset, instead outgoing partners are compensated from the profits of the business.

Should it be decided the exiting partners should leave immediately, it is still common for payments to be made to the individuals at agreed regular intervals. Sums are simply paid out following an agreed payment plan and may typically be settled over a 3-to-5-year term.

For larger regional practices, the buyer may have sufficient cash reserves or ring-fenced investor funds to complete a transaction and settle any liability as the deal requires.

Smaller SME firms will need to consider the best way to structure the transaction to facilitate the orderly migration to the new entity. This can often incorporate the outgoing partners remaining in the business for an agreed period to oversee a smooth transition of the client base.

Regardless of the payment arrangements the business must generate additional profits to meet their settlement obligations. You can understand why the points raised earlier are so important.

Bank finance for the immediate short term

The short-term working capital requirements of the new business should be understood, and if cash is unavailable then a carefully constructed funding proposal will need to be submitted to the bank to ensure sufficient cashflow is available.

A bank overdraft is a useful way to fund operating expenses (salaries, rent etc.) and where possible items such as VAT, Tax and PI Insurance premiums should be taken out of the overdraft in favour of a structured lending product. By doing this the firm can retain some headroom in their overdraft limit and still utilise alternative funding products to meet these mandatory costs.

As before, the bank will consider the affordability levels of the borrowing sums requested and make a judgment as to whether this is easily achievable by the firm.

Information required

Banks are not mind readers and therefore the bank's credit sanctioning team will require a lot of financial information. The bank's Relationship Manager is required to offer a supporting narrative and therefore it is imperative that full and clear financial information is available.

Business plan Provide an outline of the how the new entity will operate.

Financial information The last 3 years of finalised accounts including the balance sheet should be submitted together with 6 months' bank statements.

Aged debtors and creditors Provide an outline of funds owed by / to the firm, including names and the expected payment settlement dates. If any are above 9 months old an explanation is usually required to outline the likelihood of payment receipt. For creditors, provide an outline of names and amount due. Include a repayment schedule for any finance outstanding.

Personal assets and liabilities statement (used for firms with 4 partners/ directors or less) This will outline the personal wealth of the relevant persons applying for funding. This is an essential document to assess funding security.

Borrowing to repay capital accounts

It is unusual to repay capital accounts in full versus a staged payment. However, if this is required there are many lenders that can help.

All lenders will have different criteria dependent upon the legal status, size and complexity of the transaction.

For unincorporated businesses, Partner Capital Loans can be obtained so long as the partnership offers an undertaking that capital accounts cannot be paid out before the bank has received any outstanding invoice. They also ask that the value of capital account should always remain above the amount of the loan.

Limited companies are very different, and the financial performance of the company will be scrutinised by the bank. Director personal guarantees may be required, which are normally secured on a personal property.

For a practice with a good track, (strong balance sheet, profit and loss statement and operating their bank accounts to good effect) the firm will be able to secure borrowing (amounts will vary between banks) without the need for any security. Typically, rates will be between 4% and 7% over Bank of England base rate and repayment terms will vary between 10 and 15 years.

If the firm is not considered a 'strong customer' or where borrowing levels are for higher sums, then the banks will look to require security to secure funding. Even where security is taken the firm must still be able to prove affordability.

Regardless of whether exiting partners are paid from profits or funds are borrowed from the bank, the firm need to ensure the business can generate sufficient income to meet their debts.

If purchasing a partnership, understand that partner equity loans are traditionally unsecured and are supported by an indemnity from both the individual and the law firm confirming that, should the individual leave the firm, the partners' capital account will not be paid out before the bank loan is repaid.

If a high street bank will not support the request, then secondary funders can be found. This type of borrowing will be at a higher rate (8% to 20%) and security will usually be required. Security against a residential property is preferred as this means the borrowers have some 'skin in the game'.

Personal guarantee insurance protection

It is possible to purchase Director Liability Insurance, which is an annual insurance policy designed to repay the debt, rather than calling upon the sale of personal assets. This provides peace of mind to the borrower by protecting their personal assets such as the family home or life savings.

Conclusion

Finance will always be available to a well-run practice. The bank will make an initial comparison against a reputable financial benchmarking exercise. Have a clear understanding of what works well, what could be improved, and speak openly about the opportunities the merger will bring.

I cannot stress the importance of a strong culture where staff feel comfortable to openly discuss what works well and what can be improved.

Review steps

1. Understand the driving force behind the merger

2. Build a trusted merger working party – partners, insurers, bank, accountants & internal staff

3. Agree a purchase price based on a realistic valuation

4. Finalise a structured payment schedule to settle the debt to existing partners

5. Prepare financial information, supported by an external accountant

6. Ask your accountant to check projections include all future outgoings

7. Ensure business funding is in place with additional headroom for emergencies

8. Clearly explain seasonality or billing patterns to explain performance swings

9. Understand systems requirements and costs to operate

10. Complete a financial gap analysis and benchmarking exercise. Use the findings to create a strategic financial plan and regularly test and review its effectiveness. Monitor progress and keep a written record of results including changes that have been made

Remember, sound financial management is the beating heart of any legal practice. Master your approach and you will master your financial future.

Internal communication

There are hundreds of definitions of what communication means. A dictionary definition states: 'The art of using words, signs or behaviours to express or exchange information in order that you express your ideas, thoughts and feelings to someone else.' So, it is a simple act, every communication involves at least one sender, a message, and a recipient. So why throughout the merger and integration process is communication done so badly? Critical messages poorly delivered, if at all, with the assumption that all has gone well.

'The single biggest problem in communication is the illusion that it has taken place.' GEORGE BERNARD SHAW

Our research confirms this statement, simply because we all believe we are great communicators. However, the hindsight points that were made to us did not reflect that everyone communicated well, however they believed that they had.

'We assumed that staff would all be happy, communication was poor with non-fee earners and morale became a problem.' CEO LONDON LAW FIRM

You must set the style of communication at the beginning of the merger process because the way you start plays a critical part laying the foundation of the messages to come throughout the process. 'This is a merger of equals' is quite often the first message sent out, but that is very seldom the case because there is generally a dominant partner. This simple phrase sets and raises expectations for everyone – nothing will change, no one will dominate, we are all safe. Communication can either ensure success or be the reason for failure. This simple act requires you to communicate information clearly, accurately and as intended, and to engage with those you are sending the message to. The use of emails does not always convey the meaning we hoped for when we sent them, but for most of us it is the preferred method of communicating because it is quick and easy. We then assume that we have delivered the message flawlessly because we have the belief that we got it right. How often, though, do we read emails and object to the tone, which is lacking in empathy that would be delivered if we spoke to someone, and yet the person sending the email has not intended that intonation and believes that it has delivered the message as they intended. As a consequence they cause a certain tension and confusion and have a negative impact.

As the favoured way of communicating, we all receive at the least eighty emails a day, so with the volume of messages hitting our inbox daily it is very easy to overlook messages. Ongoing communication, therefore, is the single most important attribute of successful integration. There are so many aspects to consider and relay; if communication is done badly, the negatives are endless with assumed facts which are pure fiction. Once again, how you communicate must encompass how you convey your strategy and vision, convey the right message the right way with clear detailed messages that show the business case for the benefits of the merger and how they will be delivered.

The assumption that everything has been communicated well could be improved with a proper communication plan because vital messages, which we believe have been passed on, can and are forgotten with all the distractions which are going on throughout the process. Lay the foundation of what you want those messages to be, because as soon as you start discussing the merger, your communication plan has instantly gone live, and the messages must be consistent, or rumours take hold.

Communication is a skill, and it should not be just telling someone, because a vital aspect of communication is listening. Make sure that you ask for feedback and use it. There is nothing worse than believing that you are being talked at rather than to. You can be straight-talking but your language should be positive, even when you are delivering tough messages. Non-verbal communication does have an impact and can play a significant role in getting messages across. Do not say one thing, and then raise your eyes heavenward and sigh, because it will impact a person's ability to relate, engage, and establish meaningful interactions with you. Remember 70–80 percent of communication is non-verbal; inflection of your voice is often more important than the connotation of some of the words themselves. Commonly people are unaware that they are giving negative non-verbal cues but those cues are fundamental in how we convey meaning and information to others. If you sound flat and not particularly engaged and your body language mirrors that, then everyone knows you are not committed to what it is you are saying. With the Covid pandemic necessitating calls on Zoom and Teams, how often do we forget that everything we do, from posture to signs of frustration when we are unable to get our point across because the host is not looking at us, to the obvious being that we are not listening, are conveyed to others because the camera picks up every non-verbal cue.

You do not want people being territorial when they talk about the merger: in fact, ensure the message is never negative. Leave the past behind and find ways to lead the changes that are coming. You will need to be resilient and be aware of anything that becomes a barrier to change. How you communicate is the glue that holds everything together in a merger. It will ensure that you reduce uncertainty and enhances commitment to the new entity and helps you retain talent. By guiding people through a major transition you will increase the success rate of integration. If you do not communicate well, you will be the cause of ambiguity and insecurity and trust will be lost, all of which lead to a negative outcome.

Decide how you want to communicate your key messages to ensure they really are effective. There is always a fear that nothing can be said to staff for fear of news leaking externally and hindering success. However, pre-merger you can have a message ready and that will probably convey that you are talking to several parties about the possibility of merging. This guarantees that you have the control you want on merger news, and when it leaks to the press, which it inevitably will, the clear message is 'we are going to merge but we have many opportunities under discussion'. By having a simple message ready to go out you will save unease and time as you are running around trying to think about getting a message out, and what it should say.

Our research showed that biggest risk of failure lies in merger integration. The principal reason is people issues because effective employee communication is difficult to achieve as communication tends to be focussed externally.

Communications during a merger need to be clear, frequent and timely.

Be truthful, roles might be lost, your way of working will change, but do not pretend that nothing will change. Changes are inescapable but clarify why, and describe the benefits of the merged entity. If you do not send clear messages trust will be lost, and staff move to a position of fear and speculation and in their own mind they envisage worst-case scenarios, which are always far worse than reality because they are founded in fear: 'My role will be worse.' 'I will not be able to cope because there will be so many redundancies, I will have more and more work.' Of course, there will also be rumour speculation: 'I heard from someone I know that they are horrible to work for, so I may as well leave now.' Emails can be superficial and perfunctory, and enable those rumours to get out of control. Busy partners are often the worst culprits because it is easier to fire off an email than really communicate what the strategic intent is with one-to-one or group meetings. Emails can leave staff with even more questions: 'What will happen to me?' 'The partners know what's happening, but they don't care about us.' 'They hide the facts to make sure we don't leave.' Bring people together so they engage with the reality of what is happening. Staff will feel appreciated if they are included in communication messages, even if those messages are tough to listen to, because it is better to hear difficult messages in a direct way. Delivered well, staff will want to be part of the new firm. Have open sessions and listen to issues and fears that staff raise at all levels.

Communication in a merger should build momentum and enthusiasm for the merger and the benefits it brings and stamp out any myths that will predictably occur. Communication should be continuous, not an isolated event, and should always create a vision of what 'new' will look like linked back to your strategy for merging. It is better to deliver little and often to ensure that your key messages are digested and really understood before moving forward. You can build trust with interactive communication, use blogs and the intranet as a way to connect with staff at all levels.

M&A and merger integration is a long process and needs continual clarity and guidance to staff at all levels. From day one of the merged entity people should know what has changed, what remains the same, who their new boss is, where they will sit, what system changes there have been. All too often the integration stage has not been planned or communicated and staff simply do not know what is happening. Without this clarification it cannot be understood or accepted and the loss of key staff can become reality very quickly.

Great communication plans help integration and enhance knowledge transfer. Communication plans evolve as the process moves forward but they need to be monitored and refined, they are not a one-hit wonder exercise of 'done and move on'. You will be able to build employee commitment relating back to the reason for merging, even down to their own career progression. You must invest time to cascade information properly and continually sell the benefits of the merger.

Ensure that your communication plan identifies key milestones. It should include starting with 'We are in discussions with several firms because we want greater geographic reach and believe we will gain clients that we cannot gain as a smaller firm'. Let people know the name of the new firm so they get used to the change. Tell staff who has been appointed as new leaders so they know what to expect. It is vital to ensure that all key decision makers understand what the vision and message is, so everyone is aligned on the messages that are sent out.

If you have taken time to understand your employees concerns, you can continually address them in your communication plan by highlighting the changes that they believe will impact them. Key appointments will always concern staff; announce them so everyone has focus on what is happening rather than making assumptions for months.

Keep referring to key messages during the integration period and remember to highlight and articulate the reasons for the merger and why it will deliver positive change, and what that means for all staff, not just partners and fee earners.

People will not instantly recognise what will need to be done in merger integration. Give them a compelling reason and make it clear so that they see the value of the merger. 'We always did it this way but we are now doing this,' and name the benefits. This will reinforce the core messages you want to build on and will articulate the vision of the new firm and the values it will now bring.

Remember that the messages that you work on will have to appeal to a range of people at different levels and they must be refined to resonate with that group of individuals. Blogs, Twitter and videos will work better with some groups than others, but to engage with staff you must know what will appeal to them and ensure that key messages are not lost.

Throughout every firm there are staff who are influencers. Use them to cascade messages but also to ensure you know of any negative feedback, to guarantee that it is addressed quickly and head off any impending horrors, which will raise their head if not nipped in the bud.

Remember that some perceived influencers may not influence in the way you hope. Several firms told us that they were aware of 'militant secretaries' that nobody dared to upset because they were so influential. One firm had a re-education of roles to ensure they were more corporate early in the process, to ensure any influence was a positive experience not a rancour-filled diatribe.

What assumptions were made and with hindsight what was learned?

Start your communication message early in the process and ensure it continues long after the merger or acquisition has completed. Deliver key messages early in the process because it takes people a long time to understand and fully accept those messages, which is why communication is ongoing. Tailor your message to different groups of staff and vary your approach so that you succeed in getting the point home, without being repetitive and dull – you need to energise and engage people.

Leverage your intranet to help staff connect and focus. When you have team debate ensure you listen to them, and do not talk about you and how it affects you but how it will impact them in a positive way.

'Staff the tier under partners made assumptions and then developed their own belief systems, which reinforced their own false beliefs, no matter how many times we told them those beliefs were wrong.'
MANAGING PARTNER SE LAW FIRM

Your message should be clear, concise, and timely and be both internal and external. You must give clarity as to what the long-term vison for the future of the merged or acquired firm is, and it needs to be compelling. Remember that it is difficult to listen to positive messages, no matter how well-intentioned or inspiring, when your all-encompassing thoughts are fear that your role will change beyond recognition or be lost. Your communication plan should be a moveable feast and it should change as new needs evolve. Be aware of the tone you use and do not be legalistic and formal. Relate to the people your message has to reach and ensure it is not superficial. Remote working certainly needs a communication plan in place as we move from management by attendance to management by achievement.

'A merger means people start to work for a new firm but without having emotionally chosen to leave their existing firm. This tends not to cause too many issues where an individual's hierarchical position is not put under threat, but we should always expect it to cause resistance when their role is under threat.' COO TOP 50 LONDON LAW FIRM

Understand how key people are communicating and do not assume because they say it has been done that it has been done well. A well-prepared communication plan will help assure that you do not forget key and ongoing objectives.

Communication plans need to be proactive, so staff understand the process and the timeline. This is not an easy task when you are keeping your merger or acquisition confidential. A timeline can help until you can give full disclosure. Delivered the right way it will re-enforce your messages and reduce anxiety and boost morale.

All staff need to be part of your communications, not just partners and fee-earners. Staff must be able to voice opinions and give feedback; to do so they should be able to express concerns and uncertainties without fear of being talked over or talked down. An integration team with a project leader can be valuable in providing a safe environment where staff know they really are being listened to. Ensure that you respond to feedback quickly. There will be times when you cannot communicate what decisions you are going to make; you can, however, explain what the process will be so everyone understands that you are not avoiding the topic under consideration.

Senior leaders must be involved in the communication plan, do not send everything via your HR team because you are too busy. As a leader, be seen to lead from the front. Of course, you will need support from other senior executives but if you lead with a clear, strong communication plan you will engage staff because they will want to support your vision and the success of the firm.

Your communication messages must be consistent and convincing or there is no point in sending them. Communication is like planning-when you think you have done it, do it again and again. When you hear people talking about your messages in the way you wanted them conveyed you know you have got the right message out there.

Involve staff, don't let them say 'It's nothing to do with us, they are just looking to their own future profits'. Involve them in the vision, because if people are not on board you risk losing staff, and there is distress in a merger if staff leave. Think who can you afford to lose and think it through before any major discussions. If staff do not believe you, there is a communication issue regardless of if you recognise it or choose not to. Communicate at a pace that takes people with you and doesn't detract from business as usual. People can sense change and they gossip, which starts suspicion and negativity. You need to reduce levels of uncertainty when facing major change.

'Pull the plaster off quickly when there are difficult decisions to be made, do not procrastinate, it is the only way to win hearts and minds.'
MANAGING PARTNER REGIONAL LAW FIRM

Encourage staff with events that will help build a new community. Anything that will help them engage in the integration process is positive.

Case study
'We held an integration retreat for key influential staff, both lawyers and operational staff, and on the day of the launch had videos, prepared by staff to talk about what was happening. So simple, but it meant they were invested in what was happening with the merger and gave a strong message of the merged entity.' CEO LONDON LAW FIRM

'We inducted everyone, explained everything so we all started from the same point in the new firm, and no one felt they were at a disadvantage. It saved on the 'them and us' conversations.' MANAGING PARTNER REGIONAL LAW FIRM

'We ensured that we had a vision statement for staff, which was reiterated in monthly presentations, which also took into account our strategic plan and key goals moving forward.' CEO LONDON LAW FIRM

CHAPTER 8

Planning and integration

How you integrate is critical and will have a direct impact on the success or failure of the merger or acquisition. From the start of integration planning the values that will drive forward the integration are determined and will be aligned to the overall strategy of the combined firms. What synergies do you have in common that you want to build?

There are endless things to be considered that can compromise a merger deal that on paper looks good. You will have to consider potential issues like: aligning your new management team; integration must happen in addition to running business as usual not instead of it; looking at efficiencies that you have perhaps wanted for some time, and all this needs to be achieved without the integration impacting your clients. To be successful a merger or acquisition needs a significant investment in management time.

It is easy to lose sight of the objectives and the benefits they should bring if you do not have a project plan and a project director to help implement the plan. Combining two groups of people, their processes and systems and their clients is a daunting task for any management team, but a well-thought-out and executed integration plan will dramatically increase the odds of success in transitioning two firms into the one firm envisioned during merger discussions. The integration starts with a strategy and financial plan that embodies what the new firm looks like, but you need someone who can take the theory and make it reality, dedicated to the role, who will help lead you to a successful outcome.

Essential issues are sometimes overlooked. What the new entity should be called is often dismissed as something that can be done later, with the assumption that the acquirer will have top billing. Make no mistake, name recognition is genuinely important to both parties. It is said that you know you have fully integrated when people do not ask which firm you are with. Brand is important and never more so than with a merger; it has impact both internally as an expression of what the new firm is and externally for existing clients who want to support you and to help you gain new clients.

Definition of a Project Director

Ensure that you have the right resource at the right cost for the firm. People do not stop being busy because integration is going on and it is very difficult to run business as usual and integrate.

Have a project director who is accountable with a job title that reflects what they are doing in a well-defined role, empowered by management on both sides to do the job at all levels, and it does need to be at all levels. Staff from partners to support staff need to be aware that the project director has the authority to act, because to be effective they need clout.

This individual must have a deep understanding of the pitfalls M&A bring in order to pre-empt them – someone who has done the job before. Your project director and the project team will save time and pain for senior management and enable you to hit the ground running in the new entity.

They must be objective, confidential, and ethical in a time of exceptional change. Your project leader should have in-depth project management skills and organisational strength in order to unravel complex situations and bridge the gaps in culture and perception.

It is essential that the Managing Partner/CEO and project director form a strong working relationship who engender trust in one another. They are there to save you time and ensure that you can do the day job, but they will want to keep you fully informed at every step of the plan.

It is essential that they have the project team in place to work with them on the integration. People in merged firms are strangers, thrown into a joint enterprise. It is likely that only partners and finance directors have met one another. New relationships must be built and a project director can facilitate that, and it must be done at all levels, not just with partners. They will motivate and involve people and inspire them to commit to the new firm.

It is an emotive time with constant change. They need to be tough and at the same time be able to empathise with people at all levels whose jobs might be affected. They may be delivering hard messages but in a soft way to people who will be frustrated, angry, anxious and exhausted. They will take the pulse of staff at all levels.

The project director will help you create a comprehensive project plan that encompasses the key criteria to help you plan a smooth integration and mitigate risk. A detailed plan will help everyone stay focussed. They will have a clear vision of the value proposition. Above all they will help with the speed of decision making which so often stalls integration, and help you achieve your vision of the merged entity and evolve into the firm you aspired to be from the outset of the merger deal. In every merger integration there are unforeseen challenges, and you need a leader who can deal with them. You will have considered major issues such as governance, but what other issues should not be overlooked that a project director will have as part of their integration plan? Have you ensured that you have the right operational heads in place? Do you have an HR Director who can TUPE people across, who will be made redundant? Have you moved to one payroll system so there is no disruption? Are staff from both parties paid on the same day? What about benefits; have they been aligned? Will everything be in place technically, not just your IT systems? Are phone systems compatible? Has everyone changed their email address to that of the new firm and new brand? Have you aligned style of emails so footers match? Is your marketing proposition in place for the new brand? Are you pricing work in the same way or will this cause issues for clients in the new entity? Finance: have you aligned financial year-end? Is your financial strategy in line with the new firm's overall strategy? A succession of small issues can build to disrupt integration, which is why a detailed integration plane is essential.

The right project director will ensure that communication is continual throughout the firm. Informed staff are motivated because they have not been left in the dark. If they have been given open, honest, transparent and informative communication, that clear picture makes them feel involved and onside with the new firm.

Your project director should be self-confident but have few ego requirements. Their concern is getting the job done before they move on, they are not concerned with getting credit or recognition.

What assumptions were made and with hindsight what was learned?

There is no quick fix on integration. After a merger or acquisition the deal itself can be so all-encompassing there is often little appetite to integrate after the deal has been done. Whilst you can run the integration yourselves and save on costs, a project director will save you time and energy.

'It is hard to juggle business as usual with integration and transformation. The work doesn't stop and you still have people issues.'
MANAGING PARTNER REGIONAL LAW FIRM

Do not underestimate the inevitable difficulties and period of destabilisation that accompanies a merger. The best implementation programmes are well conceived and planned and every outcome considered. An integration plan has scoped out the reasons for the merger and builds on them, be that to gain competitive advantage or to gain geographic reach. Attention must be paid to all issues and the integration of human capital must not be overlooked.

'We created a merger team representing both sides with partners and multiple levels of both senior management and operational staff. The project plan contained every single aspect of what the new firm would look like from day one of the merger. Everyone knew the name, number of offices, merger of offices where they were in the same location, who would sit where, what new teams would look like, systems and process and we started to build.' CEO LONDON TOP 100 LAW FIRM

Do not undermine the authority of your project director, they represent you as Managing Partner /CEO and no one should be able to bypass them to try and influence you. Make it clear they have your authority to act in order that the right decisions are made in the process for the benefit of the new firm. Encourage the dissenters to work with not against your project director. Timing is crucial to get the project director in place early in the process so that they have a detailed understanding of the merger goals and get used to working with the managing partners. They will start mapping an integration plan before the merger is announced, keeping the managing partners and the executive team appraised and ensuring ongoing communication as the plan develops. Staff must be able to trust your project director and be able to go to them to air concerns without fear.

Get the right project director in place, a project director who has done it before and ensure that you fully support them. Get in an outsider, the right choice not a safe choice. Whilst there are many processes in any integration this individual will use a team to get into the detail whilst they continually keep sight of the bigger picture. They will help you consolidate operations and operational staff and hold your feet to the fire on time schedules and keep momentum. If things stall out in any stage of the integration it leads to failure. They are there to anticipate problems, solve them and move forward.

Do not assume because you have merged or acquired a firm before that everything will be similar or the same. You must tailor your approach, look at the cultural styles and remember all people are different, so one size does not fit all though your strategy and aims may be unchanged. Physically and emotionally instilling firms to ensure alignment needs to be decided right from the start. Both parties need to know and explore how it will work because hundreds of details must be discussed and decided upon so the combined firms can practice as one entity. Planning, cooperation, communication and patience are critical.

'We could have found better ways to expedite people integration.'
CEO LONDON LAW FIRM

From day one of the merger everything must be in place, and everyone must have a clear view of what the newly merged firm looks like. Do not wait to then try and get things in place. All too often that leads to confusion with two finance directors, two heads of HR and IT and staff either split into factions supporting 'their director' or, worse, they get tired of having no direction and leave.

You need key people in place on day one of the merger. You must have one playbook, one set of rules, one set of values, standards, and expectations. Lawyers or operational staff do not like change and any merger brings huge change, with new colleagues, changed responsibilities, a change of office involving new systems and processes.

'Appointments for senior roles were decided pre-merger. In some instances, staff competed for roles and were interviewed by a panel of partners from both firms. This process was acceptable to both parties. We ensured that those who were unsuccessful were well looked after.'
MANAGING PARTNER REGIONAL LAW FIRM

Your new management team needs to be decided upon and in place as early as possible to aid decision making. Integration will give rise to tough questions, and they must be dealt with, not avoided. Do not assume you will be able to deal with them once the deal has been brokered. Identify who your leaders will be, how management decisions will be made on legal and administrative issues because they are critical to success.

'We wanted to ensure that we were zipping together not slamming together.' CEO REGIONAL FIRM

To integrate and for those teams to see the benefit does not just happen. You need to educate people as to the benefits or the leverage of the merger gets overlooked. You cannot cross-sell if you do not understand what both sides do.

'We didn't give enough focus to the people side of things and helping them get to know one another. We got disproportionally worried about technical issues and forgot people.' MANAGING PARTNER LONDON LAW FIRM

The time it takes, and difficulties involved in integration, are underestimated at best. At worst, the integration is not given enough attention or priority because the merger deal is all encompassing.

Mix teams to help integration, do not leave them sitting in the same place in the same office in the same seats. We worked with a firm who had no planning on how teams would be conjoined. On day one of the merger both firms had the same teams sitting together exactly where they were pre-merger, so they were still two separate firms, nothing had changed.

'We had no actual integration. We took in new teams, but they all sat together as they had before, so we were still two firms, nothing had changed. We should have started with an empty building and replanned seating.' MANAGING PARTNER SE LAW FIRM

Covid certainly had an impact on any firms who undertook M&A integration during the pandemic because it stopped in-person meetings and social interaction, which made it more difficult. One participant told us that they do not find integration an issue because they arbitrarily move staff to mix things up and ensure they do not get territorial about sitting in one place with the same people.

All the firms we spoke to mentioned IT and the fact that IT integration could have been better. In some cases, one firm adopted the system of the other firm because they had already made significant investment, but the lack of planning still caused issues, particularly in IT training. It was not always thought through, so on day one of the merged firms no one knew how to open matters or set up new clients.

Post-merger or acquisition there are many important components to make the new firm come together as one, but one of the most tangible is the IT systems. It is amazing how, just 3 months before the merger, partners liken using the PMS to descending into Dante's 4th circle of hell, then post-merger they are willing to man the barricades to defend 'their' IT systems. The message must be what is best for the merged firms, not an attachment for what was.

Technology does not just contribute to efficiency, but it can also enhance communication, transparency, trust, and reliability both internally and externally. IT needs to be considered early in the process.

'Our IT team did not see eye to eye and both parties went into defensive mode. They fundamentally disagreed about the way forward. It took several months after the merger to decide who would run it. We would have been better off employing a third party because the investment in cost would have saved the pain.' MANAGING PARTNER REGIONAL LAW FIRM

'In the first quarter we expect a reduction in profits and IT is a major part of that. We get everyone onto our system and initially it slows them down. We send in our IT team to all offices with key case workers and super users to help. We also have a video suite and written guidance, but there is nothing better than actually using the system. They know how to open a file, how to record WIP, close files and prepare bills. After the first quarter the efficiencies kick in and we see recovery in the second quarter.' STEVE BULMAN MANAGING PARTNER WBW INCORPORATING BEVISS & BECKINGSALE

New buildings featured highly for many firms after the merger or acquisition and how moving firms from different sites to a new building made them feel and act part of something new. It made a monumental difference and there was real excitement. Staff became proud to be working for the firm in an environment they loved working in. One acquiring firm told us that they moved to new buildings as soon as possible because it enabled staff to let go of the past quickly as they walked into a new building with the new branding.

Other firms held partner retreats and included key operational staff directors, so the message was consistent and stopped gossip and guessing games and replaced suppositions with facts, and as a result, pre-supposed levels of uncertainty were reduced, and change became positive. Several firms we spoke to had a buddy system in place, ensuring that staff had direct access to partners and help the transition to the new entity.

Case study

The amount of uncertainty is immense in any merger. We evidenced two firms who held merger integration weekends, not just with partners but which included operational directors, so everyone was informed of the vision and how it was moving forward, timescales given and they were encouraged to cascade this into their own teams so everyone felt that they were being listened to and, as importantly, really felt part of the new entity.

We also had an example of how a firm who were moving building from three separate locations understood that it was causing anxiety with staff who had been in their buildings for years. To ensure enthusiasm for the move built, the CEO sent a monthly blog which he started six months prior to the office move, light-hearted but including facts. It was so popular that if he sent it late people would ask where it was. People felt included rather than marginalised and excitement for the move was palpable and there was real optimism about what the new firm would be like. It included when each stage of updating the new building was happening, if there were delays, which are inevitable for anyone that has moved office, he explained why, stopping any speculation. Colour schemes were explained, how reception staff would have uniforms in keeping with the new corporate colour scheme. He even told them about the new signage because it got everyone used to the new name they would work under, strengthening their brand.

Initials are often used to shorten the name of merged firms. Ensure they are appropriate. We spoke to one firm who were happy to go with that premise until their Marketing Director pointed out the abbreviation was actually rather rude.

CHAPTER 9

Planning for IT, the devil is in the detail

Key to any successful law firm merger or acquisition is the successful integration of the firm's IT systems. Whilst this may seem very obvious it is often the area where due diligence is inadequately applied, leading to a major problem for both the business and IT departments. The successful integration of a firm's IT systems from day one can provide an instant boost to the culture of the new firm with common systems, economies of scale and an agreed strategy which will give everyone confidence about future developments that match the new firm's growth plans.

Without robust planning and analyses a significant risk to the business can build very quickly, especially when there are normally different operating platforms, finance systems and versions of software running at both firms which need to continue functioning across the business from the day the M&A completes.

There are 3 key phases to ensure a successful integration of the IT systems.

1. Due diligence, to understand what systems the firms have and any potential risks, which will allow the development of a high-level idea of the cost of integration and data transition.

2. Integration plans and budget, including which systems are kept and which are not required, the staff and how the migration is going to work and what the IT environment will look like on day one.

3. The strategy going forward: what is the strategy for the merged firm? How does IT need to be shaped to meet the medium and long-term needs of the new firm?

Each phase should flow into the next one because they inform one another, with decisions made as each phase is developed, impacting on the other two.

It is therefore essential that IT is put close to the top of priorities, so discussions can begin as soon as possible at a high level between the firm's IT departments, to be able to develop an early review of the IT systems which can feed back and be factored into the viability of the M&A.

Getting together, possibly under NDA, will allow the due diligence to commence early to understand the level of technology both firms have. It's important to get buy-in at the start of this process with counterparts meeting each other. Essentially the priority at this stage is to build out the relationship and start a high-level plan together looking at the IT assets each firm has.

Assets

Make a list of every IT system you currently run along with the version number and current licences you hold. You will need to work out how the data from those systems will be migrated and a priority placed against their importance and whether there will likely be any data conversion issues.

An important first step to take when planning a merger or acquisition when it comes to your Microsoft environment is to establish an Effective Licence Position. This is an audit on the current estate to understand what risks are current and highlights any potential over-licensing. Check when the last Microsoft Audit was carried out by both firms; using this data can assist in aligning the licences. Create a spreadsheet which shows the licensing position on both sides. This will then allow an agreement on what licences will be redundant after the transition and which licences can effectively be moved across.

It is also important during the due diligence to carry out a review of the data centre and the investment each firm has made in their IT infrastructure. Consolidating and deciding where the systems are run, and from where, is vital to ensure there is a seamless transition of services.

Key points:

- Do the firms have a cloud first strategy and how far has this progressed?

- Where is the current infrastructure, on-premises, in a data centre or in the cloud, and what versions of software are currently run?

- How much does each firm spend on their current IT provisioning? Reviewing costs, contracts and connectivity is critical so an agreement can be reached early on in the planning of the system migrations; this will impact the cost effectiveness of the IT migration plan. Clearly defining and documenting this phase will allow other processes to commence and ensure sign-off on the approach.

- After the merger do the firms intend to move to a new office or will they keep or integrate existing offices? Do flexible working policies align at both firms? Since the pandemic is this an opportunity to review office space and future working requirements of staff across the business, maximising space with hot desks for flexible working? Does the current IT environment support this?

- How do staff work remotely? Have the firms provided laptops to just the lawyers or to everyone including support staff and PAs? Alignment is critical that both firms adopt the same working practices and there is consistency and standardisation in working practices. Integration is key in the early days, so everyone feels part of the same firm.

- Create a budget of the likely costs of integration and set out a price set of recommendations.

Finance systems

Thompson Reuters, Aderant or Peppermint? What do the firms use as their Case Management, CRM and practice management systems? How can you convince the finance director they might need to move to a competitor's product after a significant investment has been made rolling out a system and training staff? There will always be someone who is willing to die in the ditch over 'their' system. How easy will it be to migrate to one system, what will be the costs of breaking contracts or is one firm already in a migration phase to a later version of the product?

Again, holding a meeting as early as possible to discuss the options and views of both parties.

Always make sure you have a backup of the finance systems before the merger and that the system is available on a standalone basis for future access.

Opportunities and issues

Identify and implement a strategy which determines how the firms present their IT services. This is an opportunity to fundamentally challenge how the firms will operate after merger and will benefit from this decision. What other systems integrate with the PMS and how will data be migrated from one vendor's system to another. What reporting tools are used on a regular basis and how do the PMS integrate with other systems across the business? Don't underestimate the importance of getting this right, this can potentially be a very political area and it is vital that the discussions are conducted to gather as much information as possible to ensure it is an informed decision which can be backed up by logic and costing. An agreement reached in the early stages of the migration will give everyone confidence in the process and allow so many other decisions to be made. If doubts exist on the best way forward, then inviting the vendors into the discussion can bring around a debate internally and a chance for the right internal teams to be part of the decision making.

Identify your information management and day-to-day workflow pain points. What workflows are currently in place and what will be required post-merger? Who will be responsible for developing and agreeing any new workflows?

Are the time recording systems part of the PMS or have separate time recording products been purchased?

Software inventory

For instance, if you are running different versions of Microsoft Word then you might find that opening documents on a newer or older version will cause formatting issues. It's likely you will have a series of templates that create your house style and documents may need reformatting to include the new branded firm. It might assist if a conversion tool is developed to aid opening up documents from go-live.

Depending on the volume of documents to migrate it is helpful to work out how long the migration will take and how the conversion process will work. It's likely a document management system will be in place and an agreement will need to be reached as to how documents will be renumbered and identified in the amalgamated DM system. A challenge after any DM migration is locating your documents after they have been migrated. Has the document number changed and, if so, how can you link the original document number with the new? Consider changing the profile search screen to include a way of locating migrated documents.

A plan will need to be developed for the migration of email accounts. Timing of this is important depending on the switchover date and ensuring limited disruption in receiving and sending emails during the run-up to transition.

Often this is a good time to review the email accounts being migrated and to carry out some housekeeping and to look at any archive tools that may reduce the size of mailboxes to make them run more efficiently. By being able to reduce the size of mailboxes, it will reduce the migration time and cost.

Review all other likely data migrations, timings and how easy the data is transferrable into existing systems. In some cases, it may be that parallel systems remain in place until after the merger if this eases the IT support from go-live, but try to avoid this if possible since quite often these systems are forgotten about and just become a headache to manage later on.

It's also an opportunity to look at systems you may no longer require after the migration. However, you will need to be aware of the cost if you are breaking a contract and also the need to convince staff who are used to the system, and the rationale of why it is no longer required.

Hardware contracts

Examine how many contracts you have, any that are coming to an end or with break points which would allow for early termination. Is there any financial penalty for cancelling a contract? This will help inform you which are the best contracts to keep. Are there future growth plans where hardware such as printers, PCs or laptops may be required in the future, and it would be more financially viable to keep certain contracts running even though the hardware may not be immediately required?

What are the plans for migration? Will staff be migrated onto different laptops / PCs and if so, what would happen to the redundant kit? What is the printing strategy of both firms and how will the printers be distributed in the new environment and maintained within their contracts? Printing can be quite an emotive subject and normally law firms control how they print letterhead and continuation pages with macros. It's likely that documents may not print correctly after the migration and will need some work to streamline this in the new environment. You will need to get this in place early on with plenty of testing.

IT team and support

Uncertainty for the IT team when hearing of a merger or acquisition is the same as all support staff in the firms. Staff will immediately be worrying about their job status and how the proposed merger will impact them.

Set minds at rest as early as you can. You will need a strong team in place to ensure the migration and integration of the IT systems will be a success and run smoothly. Look at job role overlaps; do you have the right people carrying out the tasks? Draw up a departmental structure and job descriptions of roles so everyone knows where they will fit before and after the merger.

In many cases there will be duplication of roles, especially within support and infrastructure, and there will be difficult decisions to make as to who to keep. Do not put off making the decision until the merger is complete as this tends to normally lead to a team that becomes unmotivated and more worried about their jobs than carrying them out effectively.

Ideally there should be just one head of function – Director, CIO or Head of IT – who is appointed early on and who carries and delivers the migration strategy. Engage in making these decisions early since it's more likely you will have a motivated and strong team at the start.

The IT training team will be pivotal to ensuring staff are trained and prepared for any new systems or upgrades. In the lead-up to the merger prepare a training and PR plan so staff are aware of the changes they are likely to encounter. If you are moving to new offices then this process can be combined with presentations about how the move will be coordinated, and reassure staff on what to expect, when and how.

Where possible providing IT floor walkers for the first few weeks will help staff become accustomed to the new IT systems and with help easily at hand will make the transition smoother in the early days. Having a centralised faceless IT service desk will not give confidence to staff, but having someone close on hand is reassuring and continues to keep the business operating effectively should any unforeseen issues arise.

Consider carrying out a desk drop help guide explaining the areas of IT that now may be different, like the login process, accessing applications and any conversion processes that may need to be carried out when opening documents, like inserting the new logo or applying new house styles.

Include how to change your password as this is likely to be a prerequisite, how to call or send by email a service request to the IT service desk. A list of key numbers for staff also helps, especially for contacting the new and out-of-hours service teams. Introduce any floor walkers who may be on site and if possible, with some photos.

Running some training workshops in the first few weeks will allow staff to get refresher or new system training. If it appears that the service desk is receiving a lot of calls around particular applications that might be new, then make this one of the workshops so staff feel confident they are being supported and can ask questions, which in turn will improve productivity in using the IT systems.

Having 'Super Users' trained up on document conversion issues can speed up the reformatting of documents to a standard house style. If you are transferring precedents from one firm to another then carry out the reformatting in advance and check where you could encounter duplication of precedents.

Getting staff involved

Leading up to the merger and to support the IT transition try to set up a steering group with a mixture of staff from the various business and practice areas of the firm to help brainstorm the IT migration, to bring ideas for the migration plan that may have been overlooked. Briefings across the firms will help engagement and will make the transition easier knowing that staff will have buy-in and to be part of the decision making.

Security

Agree right at the start of the IT migrations who will have administration level access to the network. Make sure that with any IT redundancies the staff are not kept on site longer than is needed and access rights are removed as quickly as possible from these individuals.

In merging data are there any cyber security risks, for instance have both firms recently had a security penetration test and if so, did this show up any vulnerabilities, and have these been resolved? Consider an external system penetration test from outside consultants as soon as the migrations are complete. Is there any risk in migrated data containing any unknown threats or viruses that have not yet been detected? Agree a security plan and review that is signed off by the business before any data migration takes place.

Have both firms adopted a standard password policy and are there any weaknesses in password strength? This is a good time to review password policy, changing passwords across the business and ensuring staff sign up to new HR policies around use of the IT systems.

Risk and Compliance

Most firms have a Risk and Compliance Team, and the Director of that team is responsible for managing of all aspects of risks to the organisation, its employees, clients, reputation, assets and the interests of stakeholders. Millie Balkan takes us through the main areas that must be considered during merger or acquisition. In order to demonstrate an effective risk oversight to regulatory bodies, the Risk and Compliance function has strong links to IT to enable them to update processes across a very broad area covering a significant range of issues. Legislation and regulation are being created and amended all the time and so this space is fast moving and ever changing and is enhanced by supporting IT functions.

Conflicts of interest

Both firms' client databases must be checked against each other as soon as practicable to identify any possible conflicts of interest. If any are identified, the firms must take a view on how to resolve the matter. One firm cannot act on both sides of a litigation matter or on a conveyancing matter so the firm must stop acting for one side and communicate this to the client. Commercial conflicts may be identified, for example where one firm intends to take adverse action against an existing client of the other firm. Management must decide on how the relationship with the existing client must be managed going forward by assessing fees (incurred and expected), longevity of the relationship, reputational risk to the firm, alongside many other factors.

Client engagement and terms of business

All clients with active matters must be informed in writing that the new amalgamated firm will be acting for them and they should be provided with an updated copy of the firm's terms of business. This is a good time to review terms and ensure that the finance team are working effectively in relation to payment terms and debt recovery. The insertion of clauses in relation to cyber security and the rising threat of push payment fraud should be considered if they are not already mentioned.

AML and client onboarding / matter inception

Both firms must review their respective new client / new matter opening processes and adopt a single streamlined inception process and ensure that all staff are trained on the requirements when onboarding new clients and opening new matters. The firms may have electronic identity verification software as part of their onboarding process. If this is the case, then only one provider should be used going forward to ensure consistency with the firm's AML policy.

It would be prudent to discuss future pricing with the electronic identity verification software provider because, as the firm becomes larger as a result of the merger or acquisition, more checks will be run against new clients, so it is certainly worth exploring whether a higher volume could buy the firm lower prices for the individual checks.

Undertakings

Solicitors regularly give undertakings over the course of their work. From time to time solicitors give undertakings on behalf of the firm. All undertakings given on behalf of the firm will need to be identified as the firm may cease to exist once the merger or acquisition takes place. The undertakings must either be discharged or transferred to the name of the new firm so that they are still valid.

SRA

The positions of COLP, COFA AND MLRO will need to be reviewed and any changes must be reflected on the firm's MySRA profile.

A form available on the SRA's website must be submitted informing them of the intention to merge or acquire.

Conclusion

Being able to present a comprehensive list of your current IT estate, with licences, hardware and software assets pre-merger will demonstrate a well-run IT function and speed up the due diligence stage of M&As. As always, the devil is in the detail and the great value that a merger or acquisition might release can be undermined by a poor integration and data transition plan. It is essential that you have the expertise and knowledge available to project manage you through the 3 key phases and help guide you in making those key decisions, which have ramifications going forward on the work flows of the new firm. Whilst staff using systems do not care about data centre location or operating system, they will voice their opinions if client onboarding becomes more complicated, they cannot find documents, or the structure of their email inbox changes without explanation post-integration.

Have a strong integration plan which is communicated effectively, so staff understand what the changes are going to be. Capitalise on the new common systems and work flows, fully supported by training.

CHAPTER 10

Value to clients

One area that stood out in our research was that important client communication issues were not always addressed in the same way or given the same priority as operational issues, and it needs a paradigm shift in what you believe you have done in terms of communicating the merger to clients and what you have actually done. Some, of course, addressed the potential issues well, many others assumed it would be alright. How often do we hear the phrase 'People buy people', and everyone agreed that excellent client care will help you grow your firm's business and reputation but there was little real planning. Putting clients first is stated as a priority for most firms and is essential for future success. If you say that your clients are at the very heart of your firm, why would you not keep them informed of changes that will benefit them? One of the many issues that must be faced once the deal is signed is integration, which takes up swathes of time and energy to the extent that it is easy to forget clients, or communicate poorly with them. Your focus throughout the integration period should be keeping your clients at the forefront of what you do, or you will have a communication vacuum. This is when a strong and thought-through communications plan will be a major benefit. Having a well-thought-out communication plan will ensure that there is no miscommunication with clients and that client needs are at the forefront of the business. A project team know that is a priority and will ensure that they provide the communication plan, allowing you to concentrate on providing excellent customer service, and so that the necessary detail is worked out and does not impinge on your day-to-day business. Now is the time to show the market that you are a client-centric firm for constant and consistent client communication.

There is a significant difference between informing and communicating with clients, and sending an email is not communicating, although it might be a starting point of the message you want to deliver. Giving information is, of course, necessary and important but it is a statement.

Marketing your merger or acquisition to clients needs to take place early in the process so you can inform clients of how the outcome of the merged firm now offers an enhanced value proposition, and how you will create competitive advantage, and the benefit to them that the new firm will bring. It will follow your strategy for the merger, having different/additional capabilities that compliment your current service levels, greater efficiencies that can save them costs and wider geographic reach enabling you to expand your relationship with their firm. To do that it is essential that you invest time integrating teams in the new entity so lawyers from each side understand the people they are now working with. When lawyers fully understand that concept it is easier for them to communicate the messages you would like your clients to be aware of.

With the scale of mergers and acquisitions increasing steadily this is the prime time to send a strong communication message to clients and emphasise your commitment to them. To do that you must understand the concerns that your client might have, and that requires you to really discuss with them what they might be. However, our research emphasised that communication to clients tended to be perfunctory and assumptive.

Client concerns

It sounds obvious to state that you need to find out exactly what they might be. Did you consult your clients about the merger and the strategy you were employing or were you tempted to say nothing, justifying the reason being that of confidentiality and that nothing needs to be said until the merger is announced, and key issues decided? In our research we found that clients were told after the event, not involved at the start, and yet often the reason to merge or acquire is driven by clients' needs. Would it be a stronger proposition to tell your key clients in confidence that you are joining with another regional firm? People love being involved, and it signals how you trust them to seek that involvement and they need to know that you understand their changing needs and the issues that they are facing.

You should know how you want to develop fresh and compelling value propositions for your existing and future clients. If you can now deliver better, more efficient and broader services, show your clients the value proposition because they need reassurance that you can help them, and just how valuable they are to you.

A merger is a time when you can enhance your value by showing them your vision for the merged firm and the additional resources you can use for them. That way you can reassure them that the quality of work will not deteriorate, it will be better with the depth of experience you will gain, and the investment in technology your resources will improve, and your IT capabilities are likely to be enhanced with the merger and can give you a competitive advantage that you should be discussing with your clients.

Areas of conflict were always high on the agenda early in the merger or acquisition process, which was to be expected as firms manage conflict issues daily. Explain that any potential conflicts are being explored but that their contact will remain the same and that you will be able to introduce lawyers with complimentary experience to their colleagues in other areas that you may not have been able to assist with before. Fees may increase or you may have a different offering: clarify what will happen and do not sidestep any potential issues. Reiterate your commitment to your clients, make them aware of any key changes and ensure that you keep them up to date on what is happening because, above all, they will want to be reassured about continuity of service and business relationships. Introduce new people to them as soon as possible and suggest they spend time with the client to fully understand their business.

A highly regarded General Counsel pre-eminent in financial services said that as client businesses become more sophisticated the provision of legal services needs to move forward to keep pace. He said that if the merger altered a firm's legal ranking it was not a consideration for his firm. He wanted to know that the new entity was responsive, accurate and cost conscious.

Communication, in his opinion, is variable in that some firms have a turn-of-the-century model where the partner is the principal point of contact and no one else. That partner deals with literally everything. At the other end of the spectrum, he recognised that the partner deals purely with legal issues and the team do everything else. However, he found that the thinking is not always joined up, and found it frustrating if what he agreed with the partner does not filter down across the firm. 'Is a client a partner of the firm or a client of the partner?'

Alternative business providers such as the Big Four legal divisions look at relationships in a very different way. They have a relationship contact who may not be visible, but their job is to ensure that delivery and communication is excellent. They position the resources of the firm to address the needs of the client before the GC must ask, so it is anticipation rather than follow-up. He does not believe that firms are as client-centric as they assume in that they all say they understand the client's needs and business but that the results are more pedestrian and do not reflect what they as a client want. 'If the client is front and centre, we want reassurance, but where the billable hour rules it compromises their model for drawings. The mention of fixed fees or alternative fee arrangements is as uncomfortable to them as going to the dentist, so the proposition that they are client-centric is tenuous. It would be better if their primary focus was a different approach to fees away from the hourly rate mechanism. They believe that if they adopt alternative fee arrangements they will miss out because it will compress their profit margin. Alternative service providers take a much more relationship view and they will work on a retainer, knowing that they might not recoup for some time, but law firms will not consider it.'

Law firms convince themselves that what they go to market with is the best thing ever. By the time he as General Counsel received the proposition he said they had sold themselves into it and that it was self-evident that it was justifiable to them even if it was not what they as a client wanted.

What assumptions were made, and with hindsight what was learned?

Our research showed a gap when we asked how the vision of the newly merged firm was communicated to clients and what benefit it would bring to them. An email was considered an adequate way of telling them what was happening after the event, without reiterating why you believe the changes will be of benefit to them, to re-enforce your commitment to them. It is extremely difficult to show any kind of empathy in an email but you can certainly empathise if you are sitting with someone.

It is often the case that clients have told you why they believe a merger will benefit them and you. Now is the time to elevate your client relationship. Firms that build personal relationships will stand out. Clients like personal, warm introductions, especially when the team has expanded or if you are cross-selling. Be aware that it is easy to bombard clients with information: tailor your approach and make it feel personal.

'What message did we want to send to clients? We had differences of opinion for a long time. The devil was in the detail. We needed to evolve to get it right and that was really challenging because there were so many different ideas and opinions that it took a very long time to get detailed agreement.' CEO TOP 100 LONDON LAW FIRM

Law firms are evolving business models as the market changes, and many are moving away from the billable hour. Legal advisory businesses are entering the market eager to gain client share. The more compelling your value propositions are, your clients are more likely to stay with you after the merger or acquisition.

'It is a lawyer thing, we do the deal and move on, but how do we leverage it when the merger has been done?' MANAGING PARTNER REGIONAL LAW FIRM

Develop a plan to integrate members from both sides of the combination into as many client relationships as possible, to show your client that it is not an assumption that they will want to continue working with you and that you respect any issues they might have, and in addition you will gain an in-depth understanding of them. If you take the trouble to understand your client's strategy and listen to the clear expectations they have of you once you merge, you not only have a better client relationship, you have demonstrated an emotional stake in the business goals they have as your client. The new ways of working you want to achieve as a new firm need to marry with what your clients want, and you should not assume that they are aligned.

Ask your client questions, do not constantly broadcast on telling them what you assume they want, listen and really engage with the answers to elicit understanding. Listening and asking questions should be ongoing, not a one-off event. The value you purport to give to your client with the merger needs to be reflected in effective delivery, which is consistent.

For many clients the way a firm uses technology is indicative of their approach to investment in infrastructure and what is going on behind the scenes. If processes are straightforward and not manual it suggests a well-run firm that is trying to move with the times. The efficiencies that come with technology in the merger or acquisition show how you are trying to make things easier for your clients – innovation and technology that enhance the firm's work with them. Technology should not be a shiny thing that is new but does not get used. Show your client how it will add value and show them the kind of service you will provide to add that value.

Merger and the subsequent integration take a very long time. You need to be proactive with clients throughout and after the process. Have a central approach to messaging, make it personal and not a generic email. When you facilitate relationships ensure that those you introduce know how your client likes to work: how they like their documents executed, how much contact they like, do they have budget constraints?

Visibility and ownership of the relationship is important, and you need to preserve them. It should be an obvious point, communicate with clients well and provide an excellent client experience, and your firm will stand out. That should be a priority with a merger. At the forefront of most mergers or acquisitions is the desire to gain client work not available to a smaller entity, and to gain entry to panels. Sadly, several reports signify that whilst lawyers believe they are good communicators, clients do not always concur, and our research indicates that many law firms do not communicate with clients in the way the client expects pre- or post- mergers and acquisitions. It is a common exhortation that firms do not give clients what they want, in the way that they want it. There is a disconnect in the way value to the client is perceived. Are you giving your clients commercial solutions to business problems because you have really bothered to understand what they as a business require, and which now as a new entity you can provide? How are you going to infiltrate everyone you are introducing to the client relationship to ensure that those involved have an in-depth understanding of the existing relationship with the client, that they understand the past portfolio of work and spend? If you cannot make this connection, are you in danger of losing opportunities of showing how you can add value, and do you understand what value means to your client, or are you assuming you understand? Often that supposition surrounds cost as the most important factor to clients, but it is seldom cost alone that is important. Do you have such a strong relationship that you can challenge your client and ensure that the work you do for them is recognised as exceptional because you have bothered to find out what it is they really value? To stand out, see your relationship with your key clients as more than transactional and forge a strong business relationship where everyone involved with that client is always fully informed about matters, and really provide a relationship service. With better technology in your new entity, you can provide your client with information before it is requested on where you are with ongoing activity, workflow, and spend that you may not have been able to supply in detail prior to the merger or acquisition. This level of delivery and efficiency will show your clients how important they are to you.

Reputation management cannot be underestimated in a merger. Everything a business says and does has the power to reflect on its brand in a positive or negative way, and well-managed communication is key to ensuring the message is positive.

'We didn't have a plan on how we informed clients – we left it to individuals. That was an error as there was no strength or depth to the message.' CEO LONDON LAW FIRM

Clients can and do have concerns, and if you can answer these concerns before they arise it will show how much you value your clients, especially in a bigger entity.

'Our clients understood that the person doing their work had more support behind them, which the smaller firm couldn't offer.' MANAGING PARTNER REGIONAL LAW FIRM

Clients want personal care and continuity with their legal advisors. It is important to them that there is genuine ownership of that relationship by the partner and their team.

Nearly all contributors in the research said that they gained clients they would not have had pre-merger, and maintained existing clients, but with value add. It was deemed inconceivable that there was any suggestion that client considerations were perhaps not at the forefront of merger discussions, but communicating is about asking questions, listening to answers, receiving information, analysing responses, reassessing your position, and moving the discussion forward. In very few cases was this considered.

'We found it really challenging to decide the message we should send to clients. Both sides had differences of opinion and tone, narrative and language was very different. It took a long time to get it right.'
MANAGING PARTNER LONDON LAW FIRM

Do not underestimate the value of an independent integration team. They will release valuable time for lawyers who are busy trying to do the day job. An independent team will look at what is best for the combined firm and are a powerful tool to help you drive change. They will look at the drivers for the merger. Client feedback is invaluable, particularly post-transaction feedback, which commercial firms do as a matter of course but is not always the case in partnerships. An independent group looking at what went well and what went badly when working with clients is a powerful way to drive change. It could be something as simple as the client stating that you were technically brilliant, but the project management was dreadful. People need to get over the fear of what a client might say, and an outsider can have an impartial view that will, if addressed, enhance the client experience.

'Communication to clients was face to face. We would be stronger, have better resources and international coverage. Quality and service delivery were a very high priority.' CEO LONDON LAW FIRM

Clients should be your advocates and you should be aligned with their needs. They want your insights, they trust you and if you capitalise on that you can enhance the solutions you have for them because the new entity offers you the opportunity to craft something new for them.

'We embedded fee earners with our key clients to really understand their needs, which we were then able to assess with them and showed them how we believed the merger would address their concerns.'

MANAGING PARTNER REGIONAL LAW FIRM

A merger gives you the opportunity to educate partners of the importance of brand value to differentiate your offering. If teams do not cross-sell it is because you have not integrated them fully and they simply do not understand what they can cross-sell, so you are missing opportunities that would benefit both you and your clients. How can you gain a three-hundred-and-sixty-degree view of your clients across the firm? Once you decide how that can best be implemented for you, you will unlock collaborative opportunities across the firm, which will help you to deliver a better experience for your clients. Clients want genuine ownership of the relationship by the partner and the team. When firms get bigger, people may think it is just an institutional relationship, but clients still really want personal care, and you must show them that it will continue after the merger. If you have lost clients instead of gaining the new business streams you hoped for, you simply did not communicate well enough with them.

Do not make assumptions, anticipate the issues your clients will raise and ensure that you can deal with them.

Case study

Have you thought what message you will send to clients to ensure that you secure their long-term loyalty? I had a wonderful analogy from one participant who had brought in management consultants to consider how the merger would impact their clients. The consultancy started their presentation with a slide that showed a row of generic baked bean cans. They were told that if they did not do something well, that would be how they would be perceived, nothing different, just sitting there with every other firm. That stark image and message sparked debate on what it was the client really wanted.

Client communication really can start early in the M&A process.

'Between the sale agreement and the completion date we have three months. In that window there is a huge amount of work to be done. We send a letter to all our clients which goes out on the day of exchange. It tells them that we have

an exciting development, enhanced business, our terms will not change, and the service will be even better. We also send that to clients where matters have been closed over the last five years. We send out messages over social media and all emails have a postscript about the merger. We really use those three months to get the message about the merger across.'

STEVE BULMAN MANAGING PARTNER WBW INCORPORATING BEVISS & BECKINGSALE

What are the key marketing and business development considerations pre- and post-merger?

Although it can be easy to push marketing and business development aside with so much else to focus on during a merger, both have a crucial role to play in making sure your new firm hits the ground running.

In terms of your initial marketing and business development (BD) objectives, you have two.

The first is to define what the new firm will be, how the firm will provide a better level of service and support for your clients, how the new firm will be bigger/stronger/faster than the two previous firms and how your new firm is better than any of your current competitors. In marketing parlance this is your client value proposition.

Your second objective is to get that message out. This will involve marketing and a mix of:

- Using email, social media, and the other communication channels you have at your disposal to promote your new value proposition and your new branding

- A coordinated PR campaign that pushes the news of your upcoming merger out in both self-generated campaigns and strategically placed editorial in third party vehicles

It will also involve business development. You need to be prepared to get the message out in person to your clients and contacts. There are two reasons this is vital:

1. However attractive and well-crafted your marketing materials are, many are simply neither read nor registered by the recipients. Given how crucial your clients and contacts will be to your new venture, you can't afford not to meet up and explain what's about to happen and how the new firm will be a better fit for them.

2. Your clients and contacts (or referrers or intermediaries, depending on the language your firms use) will always be your primary sources of new work. If they are left to read about your merger, how do you think they'll feel? An important part of your business or an afterthought? With so many other firms looking to court their business and support, losing even a handful of your clients and contacts could be detrimental to your finances at what will already be a testing time.

In this chapter I'll address both objectives and offer some practical advice that will help you make sure you have both well in hand as you move towards launching your new firm.

Establishing your new firm's client value proposition

What is a client value proposition and why do we need one?
The dictionary definition of a client value proposition (CVP) is:
'A promise of value to be delivered, communicated, and acknowledged and a belief from the customer about how value will be delivered, experienced and acquired.'
But what does that mean in English?
The first thing that I'd say (and I'm mindful this may irritate or even offend some readers) is that however unique you think your firm is, there are always a number of other firms who are doing and saying pretty much the same thing. This makes it difficult for the majority of prospective clients to tell one law firm from another.

To muddy the waters further, they probably already think lawyers are an expensive but necessary evil, but this is because they don't fully understand the short-, medium-, or long-term value of the advice you'll give them. They only see the price tag.

What a client value proposition does is provide you with the opportunity to spell out exactly what your short-, medium-, or long-term value is.

Ultimately, your client value proposition will tell your clients and prospects exactly why they should choose to instruct you. It tells them what you do and how you do it. Most crucially it tells them why how you do it will be the best possible fit for them because it provides a higher level of service, value and outcome than your competitors are able to.

Sometimes when I'm working with law firms, I try and distil all of this down to its simplest form. I ask the partners to imagine meeting someone for the first time, whether that's in the office or at an event, and tell them your CVP is basically the answer to the question, 'So, why should I use you?'

Once you have that answer you will use it in person (i.e., when you meet a new prospect, and the way you present yourselves whilst writing and delivering seminars or speeches at external events), in writing (the way you structure your brochures, blogs, articles and white papers), and online (in the copy on your website and in the way you communicate on social media).

Successful marketing is consistent marketing. If everyone is introducing the firm in a different way, writing in a different way and generally saying completely different things in a different way at every touch point, it is impossible to create a credible, let alone effective, brand.

This means having a fully formed, ready to use CVP that is understood by everyone across the firm and must be the cornerstone of every firm's marketing and business development. It is even more vital for a newly merged firm.

Although you will have some cache in your existing brands, what you are about to launch is a brand-new firm with no history, no track record (outside the direct personal relationships between the individual lawyers and their clients) and no emotional buy-in.

This last point may seem a little ethereal for some, but it remains the case that people buy on emotion first and evidence second.

If you can start to lay a foundation of trust before you launch by showing your clients why what's about to come is better than what they've always had (and put your argument forward using a combination of strong marketing and personal BD), you will maximise your client retention rates.

This is brought into even sharper focus given this is the most volatile trading environment law firms have ever faced. After a year or more of working from home, clients have realised geography is no longer relevant. You can source and interact with any supplier online as well as you used to in person. Couple that with the fact that cost has become the most important factor in a purchasing decision for many individuals and businesses and it's easy to see that this is a time when clients are starting to consider finding new advisers.

This means launching with a compelling, fully formed, ready to use client value proposition will put you in the driving seat from day one.

How do you create a strong CVP?
The first step towards creating the right CVP is to work out exactly what your new firm will be, what you will offer, and how you will deliver this.

With a newly merged firm this is more difficult to find than it would be if we were talking about an existing firm going through a re-brand. You both have a name, a history, and a recognised way of doing things.

Both parties also have an established client base and an equally established marketplace, whether you define it by geography or sector(s).

This means the first thing you need to do is work out whether you want to build your proposition by taking the best bits from both firms or start from the ground up and re-establish yourselves as a brand new firm.

From a marketing perspective the first option is the easier. During your pre-merger negotiations I am sure you will have discussed the synergies and explored where 1 + 1 will equal 3 for your clients and contacts. For example, if one firm has a commercial department but was unable to provide more in-depth advice on intellectual property rights, this would be a win for your clients. Or, if you have traditionally been a private client firm, merging with a family firm could complete your offering.

Admittedly these are simplistic examples, but I trust they illustrate the point that, packaged smartly, being able to make these claims will give you a head start when it comes to creating the value proposition for your new firm.

However, a strong CVP isn't built solely on your technical legal expertise. It also needs to accentuate the service aspect of working with you. This is what will physically affect your clients, it's what they can touch and feel.

It's also what will influence your clients to recommend you to their families, friends, colleagues and professional networks.

And neither the legal nor service aspects will work in isolation; both need to be spelled out.

This is why, when I am working with firms during pre-merger, I always suggest their working groups not only include the enthusiastic marketers (and by that I mean the lawyers at all career levels who are most personally involved in marketing and BD) but also colleagues from the non-legal departments like marketing, client services, finance and reception, as they will also have exposure to their respective firms' clients and, therefore, a strong handle on what clients like, want (and don't want), and react best to.

It is this group's job to discuss what the firm is good at (and again this discussion needs to cover both the technical and the service aspects of delivery) and what clients want, ask for, and react positively to.

If you imagine those two parts of the exercise to be the circles in a Venn diagram, your client service proposition will be the common themes that sit in the overlap.

How do you use your CVP?

In short, your CVP needs to be visible in every touchpoint your combined clients, contacts, and targets will have with your new firm.

Many think the first embodiment of this will be writing the email and hard copy communications you want to send to your clients and contacts. You want these to spell out who you are and why your new firm will deliver better value and better service moving forward. This is actually the second.

I'd suggest the first use of your new CVP should be to provide your designers with a brief from which they can create your new branding. The way you want to be seen and what you want to be known for will guide their creative process and make sure what they produce seamlessly communicates the firm you want to be.

From a more practical point of view, the email accounts and headed paper you send your merger communications out on also need be sent out using your new branding, so it will need to be signed off and ready to use!

Once you have your new CVP and your new branding the next step has to be to organise an internal launch. This 'big reveal' should explain:

- Where the messaging has come from

- Where the creative has come from

- How it should be used

- The part you want your fee earners and non-fee earners to play in its external roll out

And you will notice I haven't mentioned straplines (although a strapline could fall out of the process towards the end) or 'elevator scripts'.

This is because nothing is more synthetic and less engaging. The desired outcome from this exercise is to produce a common set of messages everyone in the firm understands and can deliver naturally in their own (spoken or written) words and embody to achieve service excellence whenever they interact with clients, contacts, and targets.

Once everyone in the firm understands your messaging, they will be able to use it consistently across:

- Your written and online communications (articles, blogs, special reports, white papers, and social media posts)

- Your website's design, functionality, and copy

- Your brochures and other marketing materials

- The informal conversations your lawyers have over lunch/breakfast/ coffee with their key clients and contacts

- The more formal conversations your lawyers have at events and conferences

- Your pitches, tenders and beauty parades

- Your reception, because this is often the first thing a client will come into contact with

Again, I cannot stress just how important consistency is.

If your clients, contacts, and targets are going to react to your proposition, your proposition needs to be consistent across all these channels. Not only do people react to different media in different ways, but they also need a healthy dose of repetition to make sure your messages take root and have the desired effect (i.e. to make your new firm just as relevant and attractive to them as their legacy firm always has been).

Promoting your new firm's client value proposition

Once you have your new firm's client value proposition, you need to promote it to your clients, contacts, and target markets. We looked at the marketing aspect of this in the previous section but the most effective way to get this message out is via more traditional business development activity.

Primarily this will be via the informal conversations your lawyers have over lunch/breakfast/coffee with their key clients and contacts. This is the medium that will allow you to put over the benefits of the new firm in person, using the right language and amplifying the specific parts of your proposition you know each client/contact will react best to.

It is also the way to ensure these people feel they have been involved in the design of your new firm. This can begin before you have even formalised your new CVP.

Involving clients in the creation of your new firm's CVP
Meeting with clients and contacts to let them know you are about to merge (and dispel any fears over how this merger might affect them at the same time) is important. However, from experience I know it's also the bit that causes some lawyers the most consternation. Some don't know how to frame that conversation or what they need to say to get the people they want to see around the table.

Asking them to meet to provide some insight for a new project you are working on is a perfect reason to meet. The intrigue of being told their insight would be appreciated, without saying what for, will pique most people's interest and you should receive a cautious but positive response fairly immediately.

When you do meet you can begin by telling the person you have something confidential to share (this will make them feel valued). Once you've told them what's in prospect, you can ask them what they would promote, what they'd want from the new firm and what would separate the new firm from your competitors (people are flattered to be asked and this will make them feel more valued).

You can now leave your foot in the door to say you appreciate their insight and will be back to present the final proposition once it's available. This will make your next catch-up even easier to arrange.

'Coffee plans': The beachhead of every new firm's BD campaign

Regardless of whether you choose to see your clients and contacts under the auspices of market research in the way we looked at in the previous section, or on a more ad hoc basis on the immediate run- up to launch, this will be the beachhead-- the lead activity – of the business development element of your campaign.

The reason we call this type of contact a 'coffee plan' (and it will work on an ongoing basis, not just to support the launch of your new firm) is it involves the types of conversations that work best away from the office and independent of discussion of any open files or ongoing matters. If you are planning to meet offsite and coffee is not your thing, don't worry! 'Coffee' is shorthand for any type of drink or, in fact, lunch, breakfast, dinner, a jog, a walk or a game of golf or tennis.

The best client partners know what their clients like to do (and what they like to eat and/or drink) and the time of the day they prefer to meet at. One of the most invaluable pieces of client development advice I was given early in my career was to always match your invitations to your clients' preferences. It makes them feel they've been listened to and the psychology is if you have listened to the small details, you will certainly be paying close attention to the big stuff.

When it comes to creating a coffee plan, step one is to list out who you need to talk to. Once you have a shortlist of the clients and contacts your practice relies on you can work out who you need to see (and how/where you need to see them), who you can phone and who you can email to ask if they've seen the news and ask if they have any questions.

This type of segregation may seem a little hard-faced, but it will make the whole initiative much more time- and cost-effective while making sure you contact everyone you need to. There is nothing more embarrassing than the subject coming up months after the launch of the new firm with someone you certainly should have spoken to at the time. Again, ask yourself how you'd feel if it was the other way round.

Although there will always be exceptions (particularly those 'key influencers' among your network who may never directly give you work but are so well connected that they always have the potential of dropping your name into the right conversations) the general rule of thumb with which to assign the right type of contact is:

- **In person** Clients and contacts who consistently deliver high volumes of work, opportunities or introductions; clients and contacts who would leave a large hole in your billings if they were to walk.

- **On the phone** Clients and contacts who provide new instructions and introductions sporadically and can be counted on to provide a steady trickle of fees during a financial year.

- **By email** Everyone else. You can even make this part easier by having a set email (I save these on my desktop for easy access if I have multiple emails on the same subject to send). You can top and tail to make it more personal.

With regards to what you talk about or include in your email, you need to strike the balance between efficiency and conspiratorialism. Again, every conversation will be slightly different but very generally I would suggest you need to cover:

'**I wanted you to know first**' This is the conspiratorial element. Make sure people know you have singled them out to let them know what's happening and that you wanted to make sure the message came from you, not from the firm's marketing machine.

'**Business as usual**' You need to make sure they know nothing will change, you'll continue to be there for them, and you'll provide an updated email address, URL and any other new contact details as soon as they're available.

'**Actually, it's good news …**' This is when you go through the new CVP giving you the opportunity to stress the benefits of working with the new bigger/better/stronger firm.

'Do you have any questions?' This is an easy thing to forget but it is always a strong question to end with as it will a) eke out any lingering doubts so you can handle them there and then and in person (or by replying to their email to set up a call to deal with them if they're on the email list). It can often also prompt other questions ... the type that very often lead to new billable opportunities!

What part can formal client listening play in launching a newly merged firm?
If you really want to tackle the business development aspect of your launch by the horns and imbed your clients into the process, you may want to consider implementing a more formal client listening programme during the pre-merger process.

Of course, as this programme will have to be conducted during a commercially sensitive time, you will have to pick clients you trust and ask for their total discretion, if not request them to partake under an NDA.

Once you have an idea of what your CVP is likely to be, your clients will be best placed to confirm you've got it right.

They are better placed than you to spot holes in your messaging you may have missed or overlooked as obvious.

They may be able to give you the vocabulary and points of reference that will ensure your messaging resonates with your target market.

And remember, this part of the process is all about presenting the firm your clients want, not the firm you think you should be presenting. Taking the time to stress-test your proposition will allow you to tweak what you have before it goes public, so you hit the market with a message that addresses the direct requirements of your clients and packages and positions exactly the right client experience so:

- Your clients know they should not only stay with you but use you more
- Your contacts remain comfortable referring work to you
- You are the most attractive option to your targets

Aside from giving you much needed extra 'face time' on the run up to your launch, the best thing about confirming your thoughts with your clients is they will come at your client value proposition from a slightly different angle.

They'll look at what they – as actual clients – really value rather than what you as lawyers think they might value. They will tell you exactly how they want to be looked after as your valued clients. You can bet that if half a dozen of your most prized clients value certain aspects of your service delivery, so will the majority of companies or individuals with a similar profile.

These are the companies and individuals you will need to bring onboard to grow your new firm once your merger goes through and you are ready to begin your next commercial chapter.

CHAPTER 12

Staff considerations

'No matter how you think it will go when you tell people about the merger, look for the fear on their faces and the attitude that then comes up.' MANAGING PARTNER REGIONAL FIRM

Firms must remember that people matter, and that means all people at all levels. Of course, there will be a focus on corporate goals and ambitions that the merger or acquisition will bring, but there is seldom a merger of equals, and staff in the smaller firm not only fear for their jobs, but they also fear that their responsibilities will change and that their career development will stop. It is inevitable in a merger or acquisition that there will be job losses, that leads to a tense environment for staff and fear will and does set in. There might be an understandable resistance to change when you feel it will benefit others and not you. Now is the time to support your staff throughout the process from the build-up to implementation, which can be a long time period, and conclusion. Staff need to trust you and not feel that they are excluded or ignored because they are not lawyers. Anything they perceive is hidden, any ambiguity just becomes a fertile ground for gossip and rumour control runs rampant. We have already discussed communication and how important it is. If you want to reduce the anxiety of your staff, boost morale and retain people, do not forget how essential sending the right message is.

Tell people what is changing and what will remain the same. Keeping everyone well informed will help you integrate well from day one. Walk in their shoes and ask the questions that will be uppermost in their minds because high importance will surround what will impact them in terms of salary and benefits, what will happen to their role and responsibilities and will they actually have a job? Who will their new boss be and, if the structure of the team changes, what will that be like? If we merge or acquire and we are now in different locations, will that mean relocation?

What about their long-term career; will there be new role opportunities? Even down to system, process and procedure changes, everything causes anxiety. Everyone dealing with clients will worry about what they should say if they are asked what is happening and, if the media call, what happens then?

Have things in place on day one of the merger because that will give focus and direction rather than speculation and anxiety about what might happen.

People will often be negative initially. Sell the positives, new role opportunities, new training opportunities, better prestige now being employed by a bigger firm with a better brand proposition with the opportunity for better work, because clients who would not have come to you before now will. Remind people that a larger firm will create new opportunities and the merger and its reasons show how ambitious the firm is, and they will be able to grow with it.

'Leading a team to success requires you to own the failures'
JOCKO WILLINK & LEIF BABIN

Staff need to see strong leaders. The importance is recognised, as is the importance of the areas that will reflect staff concerns, but they often fall short when understanding how to approach them and what to do about them. Increased focus on developing strategies to better understand both culture and leadership during each stage of the merger and integration will ultimately yield stronger results. Change management led well allows the acquiring firm to communicate to employees what's happening, and how their roles and responsibilities will evolve in the new company. Appointments for senior roles can be decided pre-merger to help staff at all levels know exactly what is happening.

Several firms realised that whilst their support staff heads were good, they were not right for the size of the newly created firm. We were told that it was transformational getting new people on board.

'We thought we knew what good looked like but until it happened, we had no idea.' MANAGING PARTNER REGIONAL LAW FIRM

Get the right Operational Directors in place, Finance Director, HR Director, Marketing and Business Development Director, IT Director. In the larger entity you should have skilled professionals in place.

The **Finance Director** should be a qualified accountant, not a 'number cruncher' who has come up through the ranks, that you all know and respect and who runs so many spreadsheets they are the only one who understands them. They should be integral to the success of the new firm, by adding value to your business plans now and in the future. They will challenge assumptions in the right way rather than accepting the status quo. Technological changes and analytics tools enable significant efficiencies, leveraging data to draw out commercial insights critical to give your firm an advantage in a marketplace where everyone strives to be different or better than their competitors and gain strategic advantage. The board needs to be able to trust the financial information and debate it with their Finance Director, knowing the numbers are not ambiguous and really will aid complex business decisions and mitigate risk. Every function in the firm will benefit from a financial thought process if you have a collaborative Finance Director who analyses results and advises you accordingly. A high performing Finance Director will help you identify and articulate key performance indicators, will provide high-level management information to support and help you drive decision making within the bigger picture of your strategic business plans. As the legal market consolidates, the Finance Director is an integral part of any merger or acquisition process, particularly where firms need scale to compete. They should also be integral to the integration process. The financial analysis that they provide is a critical aid to the CEO or Managing Partner. Your Finance Director should have a combination of skills to help you meet your business objectives. The right individual will motivate and inspire not just their own team but the wider firm staff at all levels.

Getting the right **IT Director** in place is a strategic decision and demonstrates the importance you place not only on the role but the vision for the future, because the IT Director will have a strategic vison that fits the firm not just in the immediate future but in the longer term. Your IT Director will help you develop policies and procedures and use technology to enhance products and services that focus on external customers. Clients want results and lawyers who can focus their time on client matters and produce high quality work will ensure that not only clients are happy but that they remain loyal to the firm. Efficient technology will ensure that this happens, which should make it a priority in a newly merged larger entity.

HR Director, not an overhead but an integral part of the firm if they can they deliver strategic and commercial advice. They should be able to deliver a service that ensures that they have a place at the table with other operational directors. There is a fundamental difference between implementing a decision made by the board and having a full understanding of why that decision has been made, and help influence and change the outcome with appropriate solutions. Leaders within the firm are often in a lonely place making tough commercial decisions in a difficult market. They do appreciate support and you could help make these decisions easier if you can gain trust and demonstrate your contribution to the long-term outcomes for the firm that will have a very real benefit.

Marketing and Business Development are quite distinct concepts although they are deeply intertwined. Marketing is not so much a series of initiatives (such as promotion) but rather a business philosophy that puts the client at the centre of everything a firm does. It is a business process and culture that recognises the following above all else: Marketing is about the creation and delivery of client value. Business Development should help partners and fee earners focus on the strategy in order to maximise existing client relationships across all service lines and create new service lines. They will be able to help you deal with partners who have poor business development skills, be able to work with partners who are resistant to alternative ways of working, avoid potential fixation on practice areas as opposed to client problems, develop an understanding of marketing and business development techniques such as research, segmentation etc. to understand client needs and develop the right focus on cross-selling to meet those needs. For most law firms, the relationships they need to grow the firm already exist within their human capital. Investing in an automated and intelligent way to harvest those relationships will be crucial for growth in the coming years, and you need high-level staff to achieve your aims.

'New Business Operational Heads brought a totally different energy and expertise, they are brilliant, they challenge in the right way and look at things through fresh eyes. They believe in the vision and purpose so everything they do has high impact and people listen.' MANAGING PARTNER REGIONAL LAW FIRM

What assumptions were made and with hindsight what was learned?

Invest in a communications plan, focus on key messages and build momentum. Engage and motivate your staff at all levels. Motivated partners will in turn energise and motivate their teams. Morale can and does become a problem and must be addressed. Have robust and fair processes in place that champion the vision of the new firm so staff understand what is happening and why. A leader is needed to energise staff throughout the whole M&A process and well into the integration period. They will need to inspire people, to show conviction for what is happening, to be passionate and to engender that passion in their team. They need to be genuine and show how the value of a merger or acquisition will be added to the firm.

'We should have put more people together at the start, so relationships formed.' MANAGING PARTNER LONDON LAW FIRM

Sun Tzu is often quoted as 'Before you know others, know yourself.' The full quote is more enlightening. 'If you know the enemy and know yourself, you need not fear the result of one hundred battles. If you know yourself but not the enemy, for every victory gained you will also suffer a defeat. If you know neither the enemy not yourself, you will succumb in every battle.'

You will encounter hundreds of battles throughout the merger or acquisition process and if you have not engaged with staff at every level you will face defeat in areas you may not have considered. If you make assumptions throughout the process it is very likely that failure will be the result.

'We watched staff go through shock, anger, rejection and acceptance. The shock to us was that they couldn't get on the same wavelength with us and however hard we tried, they just didn't trust us.' MANAGING PARTNER SE FIRM

Be proactive and repeatedly reinforce the messages you want to get across to staff and make sure that the tone will engage them: not formal, not stuffy or legalistic and not by email – speak to them.

The facts may not be easy to discuss but do not procrastinate: communication is key at all levels to engage staff and stop resentment brewing. Make it a safe environment for difficult conversations to happen with staff because they need to know that you are listening to their concerns without talking over them. If you describe meetings as consultations you must make sure that they are. If they are genuinely consultative, therefore genuine ideas that benefit everyone will be raised. Inevitably some roles will be lost, but you must treat people with respect and compassion. Ensure that those who are unsuccessful are well looked after and compensated accordingly, and if you start this process early on, they have time to find new roles.

You need to be clear and transparent about what roles are available and what the demands of new roles will be. When staff interview for the roles available, ensure that when interviews start there are representatives from both businesses and an independent from the project team, so the decision as to who gets the role is objective and shared

'Be ruthless about having the right people in key roles, do not procrastinate.' MANAGING PARTNER REGIONAL LAW FIRM

Remember, junior ranks do have influence and can and do scupper deals. Swear them to secrecy but involve them.

'Issues weren't with senior staff but with the next level down who felt less loved.' MANAGING PARTNER REGIONAL LAW FIRM

It is common in the merger process that only partners and directors of support teams have met, so the tiers of staff below that do not feel involved in the process and feel they have no outlet for their fears and to express their concerns. One of the questions partners will ask is 'Where do I fit in?' It is no different as you come through the tiers of staff in a firm. If staff become disenchanted, they will and do walk away. If you lose your key staff your intellectual capital is drained and some of the value of the merger may well be lost. Remember that this is an emotive time for staff. Quite simply, people do not like change. They can be frustrated, angry and anxious.

'We didn't lock in key people: in hindsight we should have.'
MANAGING PARTNER SE LAW FIRM

You must stay focussed and find ways to lead positive changes. Remember, people in merged firms are strangers, thrown into a joint enterprise. New relationships at all levels need to be built and you must facilitate that to aid integration. Motivate and involve people and inspire them to commit to the new firm. Be aware that it is easy to focus on the merger deal and ignore the people who are your most valuable assets.

'You need to integrate rather than infiltrate staff.'
MANAGING PARTNER LONDON LAW FIRM

Use innovative ways to engage your staff and get them involved in getting critical messages across to team members on the same level. Use blogs, videos, anything that they will tune into. A video of the new office and how it is developing is much stronger than an email telling them how nice the new building is.

If staff do not believe you, there is a communication issue regardless of if you recognise it or choose not to, and if staff are doing their level best to cause issues, they either do not believe anything you have told them, you have not communicated well, or perhaps they had no place in the new entity and you should have tackled that early in the process. Did you start communication early in the process and did you ensure that it was constant, clear, concise, and timely to staff? Did you remember that communication does not stop once the new firm has been announced, it must carry on throughout the integration stage?

If your Operational Directors cannot cope with the requirements of the new firm, that is not their fault, you should have considered what staff you needed at the start of the process. If any of your operational staff are arguing because you have two Finance Directors, two HR Directors and two IT Directors, this is an issue you should have owned and had the right people in place on day one of the merger.

If you lost staff you really wanted to keep, why did you not give them the vision of their place and career path in the merged firm? Was it because you assumed everything was alright?

'The loss of staff was painful and that caused tensions in the shareholder group.' MANAGING PARTNER REGIONAL LAW FIRM

Do not let frustrations build as people get used to working in a new team with new colleagues in a new way. Integrating people is vital to success, so help them and do not assume it will 'sort itself out'. Get them involved by having team meetings, lunches, champion anything new with videos and talks to ensure engagement.

'We could have found better ways to expediate people integration'
CEO LONDON LAW FIRM

Case study

We heard of different ways to ensure that staff were engaged with the whole process of moving office and not entrenched in their old building. One firm sent a weekly blog for six months prior to the move. It was informal, humorous, and light-hearted but it also contained facts about the building and the phased move. In that way staff felt engaged and very much part of something. Certainly, an office move ensured that teams were joined together, seated differently to benefit everyone and properly integrated. A common statement was that as soon as you get people out of old buildings they feel and act part of the new entity.

'We knew staff had to be a key consideration. From day one we had a project plan in place, which contained every single aspect of what the new firm would look like. We made sure everyone knew who would sit where, what their new team would be like, and we started to build. As much as possible we did face-to-face meetings and engaged with staff at every level to secure their loyalty and give them a sense of identity in the new firm.'

As soon as we exchange, we have a clear programme of how we are going to make things work. In the first week we visit every office and meet all the staff. We answer immediate questions, we reassure people, and we tell them about us. HR send out a questionnaire; it asks questions so we can really get to know people.

This includes questions about what work they do, what their IT skills are, any grumbles that they might have, and which office they work in. This goes on to the HR system so Heads of Department can access it and get to know people. With our latest merger we had four new offices, so we asked new and existing staff if they wanted to move to a different location. It has been really successful for all our staff to move around because they share information, ideas and views and they are keen to integrate. We also send a weekly update to all staff, which includes a merger task list so everyone can see what we are doing. People feel included and important. We do not want to lose goodwill and confidence of our staff.'

STEVE BULMAN MANAGING PARTNER WBW INCORPORATING BEVISS & BECKINGSALE

CHAPTER 13

What did we learn?

With the gift of hindsight, what was learned in the process? All the firms we spoke to were happy to share the good, the bad the shockingly unexpected and the exhaustion that comes in the merger process, so we have given priority to their thoughts throughout the book. At the start of the research we wondered what, if any, themes would be repeated and would we gain any better understanding of the errors that replay in M&A, particularly when it comes to the integration part of the process, which is where so many firms fail. Firms we interviewed in November 2020 and firms we have questioned in mid-2021 relayed exactly the same issues.

Many weighty tomes have been written and we wanted this to be about personal experiences that others can benefit from, and certainly distinct themes did emerge, and yet we all carry on making the same mistakes. Whilst undertaking our research someone told us that they had thought of similar issues twenty years ago but here we are, two decades on, and they are still happening.

John Fletcher the playwright stated: 'Of all the forms of wisdom, hindsight is by general consent the least merciful, the most unforgiving.'

We hope this research helps you to use that wisdom because if we listen to our peers, we can benefit from their gift of hindsight and the painful lessons they endured and the failures they have encountered, as well as things that stood out to make their experiences better. They have given their time to save you hours of your time because they have faced countless problems and they have learned from them, and so can you.

Firms that stated that it went well and there were no learning points we believe could have done better because we have the benefit of hindsight, gained through our research.

From the beginning

There is no right answer or 'one size fits all' in how to make a merger or acquisition and the subsequent integration work, because it must be appropriate for you and there will always be bumps along the journey, which will sometimes feel like mountains to overcome. It takes an immense effort to make it work. Being aware of the pitfalls that you will encounter will help, and an experienced Project Director will give you a major advantage to help you prepare. They will start with clear objectives, and a project plan that will help you prioritise issues to move the plan forward. They will save you time and smooth the journey throughout the integration. You will learn how necessary it is to build, layer and clarify plans to aid success. If you do not, then failure looms large. Those firms that failed to secure a merger partner at their first attempt fell into three distinct camps: those that did not try again, those that tried again but had a similar result and those that used the opportunity to reassess their capabilities. Those that reassessed often brought in an outsider to see why their potential merger partner walked away, which enabled them to dig deep, however uncomfortable that journey was, to understand what they needed to do to get into better shape to attract a merger partner. An external advisor can help you challenge your thinking and confront areas where you can improve.

If Managing Partners shared their vision for the merger as still being a well-planned strategy, they then were able to look at how they could improve.

Was their lack of profitability putting off potential merger partners, did they make their people more accountable with KPI's and targets, and can you learn from that? Were they locked into an equity arrangement that the other side thought old-school and that they had already changed, leaving them without the appetite to go through it all over again? Once they addressed the issues raised by their external consultant they were able to go back to the market with an improved choice of potential merger partners. Your Project Director will not think in terms of bending the shape of the issues to fit a potential deal with friends. They look at everything factually to help you realise your vision.

Have a strategy for merging. Do not enter a merger on the gut instinct of two individuals who know one another and who wholeheartedly believe it is an exciting deal, because you can become so invested in the excitement of chasing a merger that it is easy to make a bad decision. Ensure that thorough due diligence and analysis is done to support the facts and it might still be an exciting deal; just make sure it is one without hidden surprises. Start as if you are building a firm from scratch, looking at every detail to see what improvements can be gained, re-evaluate everything. Sometimes Managing Partners want a deal and drive towards it, but their own partners might not be ready to take that step forward with them. Just because you might secure a deal, it does not follow that your partners will automatically be on side and receptive. If partners decide to disrupt the merger integration once the deal has been signed, what did they not believe, and why did they not trust you? You did not convince them that the merged firm would be better than the two individual entities.

Many of the issues we heard are avoidable. If staff do not believe you, there is a communication issue regardless of if you recognise it or choose not to. Staff at all levels can disrupt mergers for sundry reasons so it is crucial that you find ways to be open and honest when you enter any communication. Remember that people fear change and become anxious about new teams, new ways of working and their new boss or loss of power.

'We assigned partner mentors to get the newly formed teams up to speed and anchor people into the practice areas.'
MANAGING PARTNER LONDON LAW FIRM

If staff are doing their level best to cause issues, they either do not believe anything you have told them, you have not communicated well, or perhaps they had no place in the new entity and you should have tackled that early in the process. If one side continually refers to you as 'that lot', they have not been shown the value of the merger and what it could mean to them, so they had no sense of unity. If teams do not cross-sell it is because you have not integrated them fully and they simply do not understand what they can cross-sell, so you are missing opportunities that would benefit both you and your clients.

If your Operational Directors cannot cope with the requirements of the new firm, that is not their fault; you should have considered what staff you needed at the start of the process. If any of your operational staff are arguing because you have two Finance Directors, two HR Directors and two IT Directors, this is an issue you should have owned and had the right people in place on day one of the merger.

Invest in getting the best staff in key roles to make a fundamental difference in the new firm. Remind people of the reasons for merging. So often we were told it was to gain hires that could not be attracted in a smaller firm.

'We had new business heads who were legacy agnostic and they had power, so people listened. Through their experience and expertise and energy they look at things through fresh eyes. They really believe in the vision and purpose and everything they do has high impact.'
MANAGING PARTNER REGIONAL LAW FIRM

'The merger enabled us to recruit lateral hires that we just would not have been able to before we merged.'
MANAGING PARTNER SE REGIONAL LAW FIRM

If you have lost clients instead of gaining the new business streams you hoped for, you simply did not communicate well enough with them. If you lost staff you really wanted to keep, why did you not give them the vision of their place and career path in the merged firm? Was it because you assumed everything was alright?

Cost savings imagined or real came up. We could do it as well as an external project team and without the cost. Major firms can and do, but the smaller and mid-tier does not have the resource necessary and smaller firms learn quickly how utterly exhausted they became trying to deal with business as usual, bill, ensure staff issues are dealt with and then muster the energy needed to deal with the endless details of the merger and integration.

Timing is always difficult and usually takes longer than anticipated as you work your way through regulatory issues, compliance, dealing with banks and insurers.

Merger integration is complex, hard work and brings people to their knees. Once the deal is done, mergers fail so often because partners running it cannot face the barrage of decisions that have to be made and the constant need to keep everyone on side as the integration starts.

'People just didn't understand the amount of effort needed in integration.'
MANAGING PARTNER REGIONAL LAW FIRM

Clearly central cost efficiencies are important after a merger but there are always integration costs which must be considered with a clear financial plan. Cost savings on marketing and PR, swept aside because clients know and trust the firm. They did, but will they be moving forward or are you assuming they will? Did you communicate with them or did you just tell them you were merging and assumed they would be impressed? 'It was not as successful or as profitable as we had hoped' was a common refrain. Did you have a strategy beyond the merger and how did you plan to drive it forward? Don't make marketing an afterthought. Invest in the function and use it to its full and proper potential.

IT costs not thought through and not costed by an outside expert. As a result, two systems are run, each side proclaiming theirs is better. Often two IT Directors fighting for different concepts. The cost of a new system is often seen as prohibitive to partners who do not have the appetite to invest. Perhaps it is because that 'hidden cost' was not explained to them, and they now see it as a cost they do not need or want, and which impacts their equity. Ensure that the costs of the merger do not outweigh the benefit.

Have strong and effective leaders

'I was a better leader once I had done my MBA, I looked at things in a more commercial way, which benefitted the business.' MANAGING PARTNER REGIONAL LAW FIRM

Mergers and the following integration need great leaders who are passionate about what they do, who can adapt to the needs of the firm and empower and develop their teams because they are confident about the people they have brought in to manage key areas of the firm. The right leader will be ambitious for the firm not their own glory. They will motivate and inspire staff and as a consequence they will earn respect. Do not be afraid of hiring people that may eventually be better than you.

'I can clearly see a succession plan to my role as CEO because I have ensured that there are quality staff to choose from. They simply were not there before the merger.' CEO LONDON LAW FIRM

Leaders have to make hard choices and there will be plenty that need to be made throughout the merger and integration process. They do not shy away from making tough decisions and they do not sidestep them by seeking consensus on the decisions that are difficult.

'Working with a business coach and mentor opened my eyes to leadership.' MANAGING PARTNER LONDON LAW FIRM

Ensure that your operational heads are of the highest quality to help you manage the firm's performance and individual contribution.

'It was a feather in my cap to get the best people on board and, frankly, they make me look good because they add so much. They are the key to success moving forward.' CEO TOP 100 LONDON LAW FIRM

Make sure that the culture you have engendered is lived by those working with you because it will enforce the values of the business that make you unique.

'Friendships were formed on a vision that was better than both legacy firms. We have tight leadership that is positive about things. Because our leaders were close, we quickly thought of ourselves as one firm. If that doesn't exist you have rivalry and competitiveness about things.' MANAGING PARTNER REGIONAL LAW FIRM

Several participants mentioned that whenever firms come together there is a fear amongst partners of a loss of authority and their roles changing. However, one Senior Partner explained his change of role as 'wonderful' because it allowed him to do what he loved, and he did not have to worry about day-to-day issues.

'One day a new printer arrived at the office, and I told the delivery people it must be an error. I was told no, it was all sorted, and they installed it.

Now when I was Senior Partner I would have to present a case for having new equipment and there would have been days of debate before we moved forward. Now I do not have to worry about it, it is done, and I just see the benefits.' GERALD SHAMASH EDWARDS DUTHIE SHAMASH

LLP considerations

Strengthen your LLP agreement. This will help you protect and stabilise the business against the risk of departing partners. The success of the merger depends in part on you keeping your best performers. Your LLP agreement can help you be very specific about the obligations partners have to the firm, and may help act as a deterrent for those who are thinking of leaving and taking their team with them. Include safeguards covering the firm's confidential information, and a requirement to notify the firm if they receive a job offer.

One seldom-used provision is **The waiting lounge**, designed to stop the issues of multiple and simultaneous partner departures. A 'waiting lounge' provision is designed to tackle this by preventing more than a specified number or percentage of partners from leaving during a specified period.

Restrictive covenants to safeguard the firm's goodwill, restrictive covenants applicable to former partners need to be reviewed to ensure that they are enforceable under the current law.

Garden leave enables the firm to lock a partner out of the business during their notice period and gives the firm the opportunity to consolidate and transition client relationships.

Good/bad leavers these provisions can encourage good behaviour by departing partners (e.g. compliance with restrictive covenants) and penalise those who breach their obligations by deferring any payments due to the bad leaver over a longer period or offsetting any damages suffered by the firm against the bad leaver's financial entitlements.

Notice period for voluntary retirement: consider whether the current notice period is sufficient to protect the business. You cannot afford to lose high performing partners during or just after a merger. If they exit you will lose capital and have the potential of losing existing and potential clients.

Due diligence

So many participants in our research started the merger process by going to firms they knew and having informal chats. They asked clients what they thought of the firm and looked at press coverage to see how the potential merger partners were perceived, and sometimes spoke to peers to establish if they knew any of the partners, and what they were like. A broker can help you deal in facts about the potential partner and not concentrate on an emotional connection that obfuscates truths you would rather not consider. Your broker should have a breadth of knowledge about your potential partner. Informal due diligence gathered is inexcusable and the reason so many mergers do not go to plan.

Conduct thorough due diligence across every area, not just finance. Has EBITDA been calculated appropriately? Are there any staff disputes? Have you considered technology licences? Have a long look at contracts with suppliers and PII. Are there any settlement agreements outstanding? Do not leave things to a 'gentlemen's agreement.' Lack of due diligence in PII for many had hidden issues. Time and again our research showed that fractures opened and often took years to heal, if they healed at all, because of poor due diligence.

There are firms who really ensured that they covered all areas of due diligence thoroughly. One participant conducted an audit on live and historic files. They looked at procedures and themes in work, analysed claims and complaints to check the quality of work undertaken. To ensure confidentiality their teams went in over a weekend and had a standard form to complete on given areas. They looked at engagement letters, attendance notes and communication with clients. Regarding finance they looked at historical accounts information and working capital management. Their due diligence covered everything regarding office management – anything from contracts on photocopiers to IT, to see which contracts could be brought to an end, if at all. The acquiring firm made a contribution to the termination of contracts, but the termination costs remained with the previous LLP. Storage was examined; was it on site, off site in a specialist unit or on an industrial estate where the building was leaking and falling down? They assumed responsibility for storage for eighteen months post-deal and it reverted back after that given time period. They checked file closure procedures and destruction processes, all part of the deal as the successor practice. They did not want to take over files that were not closed but were completed. An internal resource was given a project to deal with this issue. They admitted an error in hindsight that the individual leading this project had already been served notice so his attention to detail was poor, he was leaving, why should he care? If they had sorted his departure out later and kept him in place it would have been more effective than the money spent unpicking the mess he left behind. One participant told us that as part of their due diligence they did not just look at the lawyers who are there, because they know what they are getting, not what you are buying. They conducted due diligence on those who had left within a given time period from a liability standpoint.

'When you check files remember that lawyers are trained to pick things apart, so you are never going to find that everything is perfect. When looking at files the issue is not 'are they best practice today?' but 'were they best practice at the time?' What someone did five years ago will not necessarily be how they do things today. Judging yesterday's advice by today's standards is often to look only at the negatives and so find an often-unjustifiable reason to walk away.'
DUNCAN JACKSON CEO BUCKLES LAW

'Our due diligence should have been better but as the acquiring firm we were worried about upsetting the firm we were acquiring.'
MANAGING PARTNER REGIONAL LAW FIRM

'We asked about PII claims and we couldn't find any. It was only when we merged that we found out that was because claims had been paid off, but not through the insurer.' MANAGING PARTNER SE LAW FIRM

What's in a name?

Whilst deciding a post-merger law firm name might seem a bit trivial in comparison with negotiations over client conflicts, remuneration, partnership structures and property conundrums, getting the branding right is crucial for the firms' staff and clients alike and internally it can cause major disagreement just at a time when you think everything has come together. An explanation for that reluctance can arguably be found in the inherently political nature of partnerships. When dealing with an organisation of multiple owners, decision making is tough at the best of times and it is exacerbated because of hundreds of decisions that must be made throughout the merger integration process. Opinions over a law firm's name can be highly emotive. People want to hang on to the history of the name which clients know and are drawn to, partners have emotional attachment to it and, when so much else they held dear has changed, they battle for the name. Often the name relates to founding partners who have long since departed and are unknown to anyone in the firm apart from the name. Is it a good idea to have a string of long names, and do they work when we think of all the digital platforms your firm's name will be used in, which is why they eventually get abbreviated to initials and then are dropped altogether? Merged firms often opt to keep a long name that is simply the combination of the legacy firms for a year or so before gently dropping elements, or they use both names linked by 'incorporating'. The rationale is that the process gives the merged firms and their clients a chance to get used to it after the merger and that they do not need yet more change. This, however, could be the ideal time to change name and brand because you have created a new entity. Inevitably there are those who fear change, and for them the greatest change will be in losing the long-standing firm name. The process can be managed far more effectively, with a communications plan that integrates the new name into your planning Major commercial firms do this so effectively that the brand they decide on dominates. Who has heard of Blue Ribbon Sports? Very few, but we all know Nike – they had fourteen years as Blue Ribbon, but clever re-branding promoted the new name. What about Brads Drink? not catchy, but Pepsi is known globally, and Amazon started life as Relentless, which most of us have never heard of, let alone connected with, and we do not care because Amazon is the name we all recognise, as Jeff Bezos had a vision for what he wanted the business to become.

In the legal sector we get entrenched in the history and how we cannot do without a name because of its connections, rather than focussing on what we might achieve if we re-brand. We take the cost of re-branding several times because we feel we must, for fear of upsetting partners and clients who will no longer know who the firm is. We fear loss of the past that we have put behind us when we merged. We would rather start with a long name wait, lose a name or two, wait and then abbreviate to initials and announce it as though it was special. Would it be better to say we have merged, we are proud of it and we are going to be known as Z, and have that in your planning at an early stage, even if that designation is part of the original firm's name.

Clients will be maintained, and new clients won, if they know the name you are moving forward with. If you have a new entity, make everyone proud of it rather than harbouring what was, and concentrate on what is. If that includes any part of the name, then promote that from the start. Major acquirers in the market do not even consider maintaining any part of the name of the firm they take over, they brand from day one to maintain their identity and get buy-in from the acquired firm and staff so they feel part of something new.

What is success?

From the vision you started with, was it successful? This was our final question to participants in the survey, and we heard cautionary tales about merging and a lot of doubt about the success, however compelling the original strategic argument if there was one. You need to be realistic about post-merger economics and the time it takes to achieve your objectives. Our research reflected that most firms take 3-5 years for everything to settle down. Others said that everyone in the firm measured success in different ways. The Managing Partner looked at profit and turnover as a measure, some of his partners looked at integration and how their teams were cooperating, were they are getting on and were people happy?

Those that remained true to their criteria for merging saw success. Those that looked at the merger as an opportunity to adopt and re-evaluate how to change so there was improvement for both firms, and who saw it as wholesale transformation, saw the greatest success. Sadly, the majority said it had not fulfilled expectations. It was universally agreed that any merger or acquisition needs proper resource and careful planning. The firms we spoke to believed that they had followed that principle, but their hindsight comments did not always follow the same logic, with many of them saying that there were no learning points, whilst in the next breath stating how sad they were when they lost key staff who took a long time to replace, or how difficult partners were. It is certainly a delicate balance to get the innumerable issues right.

A merger's success can take years to really bed in and firms must be pragmatic about that. Rather than wondering how successful it was, how could you measure that success? Check your key criteria for the merger or acquisition. Are your partners making more money? Do they have new clients? Do your clients think you are offering a better service? Did you extend your geographic reach? Are you offering a career path to staff you were unable to previously, and have you attracted better quality staff?

Time will tell because we only see success after it has been reached.

'If you look closely, most overnight successes took a long time.'
STEVE JOBS

There is no right answer in M&A, there is no 'one size fits all', because it has to be right for you.

Acknowledgements

First of all, a huge thank you to everyone who agreed to be interviewed and who gave me access to a range of stories and issues exactly as they had faced them. To everyone I reached out to and asked if they would share their contacts and so introduce me to firms who had been through the M&A experience, I appreciate your generosity. It is only through all these people that the book was formed.

My co-contributors who have added their expertise and support over many months and who when asked to hit the deadlines I imposed did just that. To my husband who indulged my hours of writing, interviews and perhaps the odd tantrum as I strived to encapsulate everything shared with me at the cost of most other things.

It has been a privilege and if anyone sees this book as it was intended, to form a practical guide, a real go-to directory from your peer group for all issues in M&A that will enhance how you go about the process and that will help you avoid errors, then we have all been successful in what we started out to do.

Printed and bound by CPI Group (UK) Ltd, Croydon, CR0 4YY

09/12/2024

01802714-0001